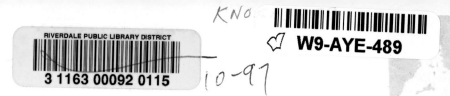
Do-It-Yourself Decorating
Step-by-Step
Stenciling.

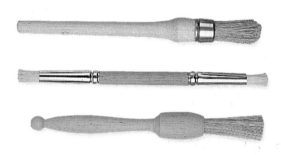

Paula & Peter Knott

Meredith® Press

Des Moines, Iowa

Contents

Introduction 4

Ideas and Choices 6
For the bedroom 8
In the kitchen or bathroom 10
On almost any surface 12

Tools and Materials 14
Types of stencils 16
Stenciling equipment 18
Paints and materials 20
Applicators 22
Caring for tools 24

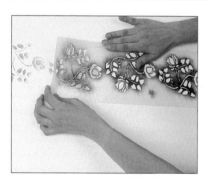

Basic Techniques 26
Positioning stencils 28
Using stencil paints 30
Using stencil crayons 32
Stenciling large areas 34
Correcting mistakes 36

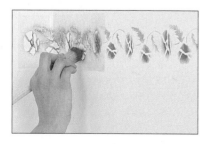

Surfaces to Stencil 38
Base surfaces 40
Walls 42
Doors 45
Floors 48

Furniture 50
Fabrics 52
Tiles 56

Projects 58
Room friezes 60
Grouped stencils 62
Blinds and lampshades 64
Rugs and mats 66
Fire screens 68
Containers 70
Cakes 72

Creating Illusions 74
Plate shelf 76
Hanging basket 78
Garden balustrade 80

Designing and Cutting Stencils 82
Single-layer stencils 84
Multiple-layer stencils 86
Using a crafts knife 88
Using a hot-knife cutter 90

Glossary 92
Index 94
Acknowledgments 96

Introduction

We've written this book to give you all the information you need to stencil a variety of surfaces.

Stenciling can simply highlight a corner or decorate a favorite object, or it can create an all-encompassing effect as a floor design or a complete wall treatment. In the "Ideas and Choices" chapter (page 6), we'll help you choose the right effect and subject for your project.

You probably already have most of the tools and materials you'll need. In the "Tools and Materials" chapter (page 14), we also show you some that are specific to stenciling and give you tips on caring for your tools and equipment.

You first must accurately position your stencils, then apply paint to them in the way that's best for your project. In "Basic Techniques" (page 26), we cover the skills you'll need for any application.

Stencils can be applied to almost any surface. We cover the paints and techniques you'll use to decorate walls, doors, floors, furniture, fabrics, and tiles in "Surfaces to Stencil" (page 38). In the "Projects" chapter (page 58), we show you how to stencil a variety of specific items, from blinds to cakes.

The "Creating Illusions" chapter (page 74) gives you ideas and practical solutions for transforming a room using brushes or a sponge and stencils. Your design possibilities become almost limitless when you make and cut your own stencils. We show you how in "Designing and Cutting Stencils" (page 82).

Ideas and Choices

Choosing the room to stencil, the surfaces to decorate, the design to use, and the color scheme to try gives you a mind-boggling number of options. Here's some inspiration—a variety of rooms and surfaces to help you plan your own designs. In some cases, the designs are picked up from fabrics in the room; others use several stencils with a common theme; and still others adapt part of a room design to use elsewhere or add humor with trompe l'oeil, or fool-the-eye, effects. Don't limit your use of stencils to inside the house. They're equally at home cheering up exteriors—from doors and window boxes to garden sheds.

This chapter contains

For the bedroom	8
In the kitchen or bathroom	10
On almost any surface	12

For the bedroom

You can get your stencil designs from bedding or curtain patterns to create a theme. Position the designs high or low on the walls to change the apparent shape of the room, or use them as a border to show off a pretty window, decorative headboard, or piece of furniture. By using a single motif but mixing stencil shapes, you can let the walls of a child's bedroom highlight a favorite hobby or sport. When interests change, it will be simple to update the design by painting out some areas and adding new stencil motifs.

▼ These door panels, decorated with flower-design stencils, appear more striking because not every panel was stenciled.

▶ A space bordered by beams is an ideal spot for a single stencil. The design was taken from the curtain fabric.

▲ Enlarged from the curtain fabric, this geometric design was used for a wall border that echoes the colors in the fabric.

◄ Stencils are easy to change. These motifs can be painted over whenever new ones are desired.

► A variety of designs with a similar theme make an exciting mural, such as the kinetic scene shown here.

► Making your own stencils lets you picture anything you want—even a favorite sport.

▲ The rough surface of the wallpaper above the picture rail called for a bold stencil here. Fortunately, the bedspread provided the inspiration.

▲ Sisal carpet gains immediate interest teamed with a broad stenciled border. A final light spray with a soft sand color produces muted shades.

In the kitchen or bathroom

Most kitchens and bathrooms include large areas of hard, single-color surfaces to which stencils can lend a natural decorative contrast. Introduce pattern around windows and on walls, floors, tiles, fabrics, and accessories. Seaside or water motifs turn a bathroom into a delight, just as stenciled fruits and vegetables add to the culinary ambience of a kitchen. To protect stencils in these hard-use areas, cover the finished designs with varnish.

◄ The glazed fruit-design tiles on the wall and the china were the inspiration for the fruit frieze above the kitchen cabinets.

◄ Ivy replaces a cornice to border this window top, and a single stencil fills the front of the range hood.

▲ Stencils that are applied to dark-colored backgrounds should be painted first with white. This is what gives such vibrance to the flowers on these dark kitchen cabinets.

◄ A variety of seaside-motif stencils dots the walls and floor of this bathroom for a whimsical nautical effect.

▼ Even a plain shower curtain can be transformed with a stenciled design when the colors complement the room scheme.

◄ Stenciled motifs coordinate beautifully on the walls, floor, and accessories in this bathroom corner.

► Crossed cutlery is decoratively symbolic above the pass-through to this kitchen.

On almost any surface

The many different types of paints used for stenciling let you decorate a surprising range of surfaces—interior walls, floors, furniture, fabrics, and tiles. Even in a greenhouse, you can use stencils to add exotic plant species that never need watering or suffer from disease. Use stencils outdoors, too, where they transform garden walls, fences, and patio furniture. Hide or highlight a garage or shed with a garden theme, or use decorative stencils to label flowerpots with pictures of the plants they contain.

◄ The garden-shed border was created with nothing but stencils, masking tape, three colors of paint, and a sponge.

▲ Any room looks like a greenhouse with extra potted plants courtesy of stencils.

◄ A potting shed is treated to a stenciled lion's head.

► Fruiting and flowering lemon trees adorn this garden room.

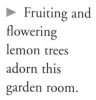

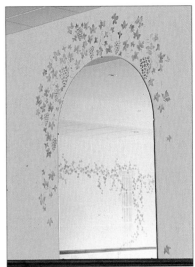

▲ The curved shape of a hall mirror is enhanced by a delicate frame of grapevines used asymmetrically to echo nature. The stenciled walls opposite are reflected in the mirror.

◄ A mock stone, ivy-covered border transforms a summer house with stenciled views from every direction.

▲ A stone canopy design above these doors turns an unassuming entry into a prominent feature of the room.

► This modern cupboard could be mistaken for an antique with its dark colors and folk-art-design stencil decorations.

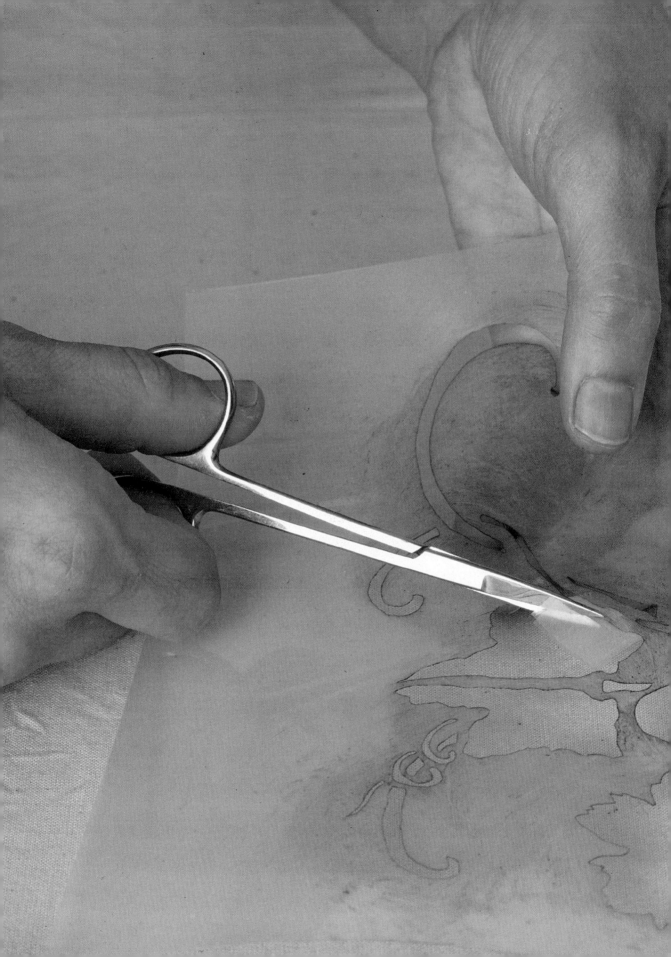

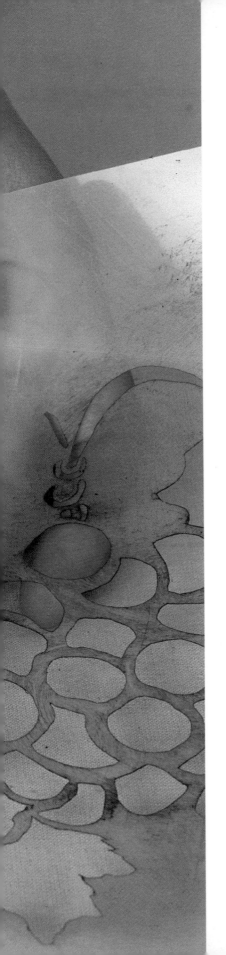

Tools and Materials

Buy the best quality tools and materials you can afford. If you take care of them carefully—cleaning them immediately after use, repairing them when necessary, and storing them properly—they'll last a lifetime. Good tools also make it much easier to get good results. Few tools and materials are unique to stenciling; you probably already have a number of the items shown in this chapter. Most of the general tools and equipment shown here are available at hardware stores, home centers, and office supply stores. Other less common items are sold at art stores, graphic design outlets, and crafts stores. Just keep looking, and you're sure to find what you need.

This chapter contains

Types of stencils	16
Stenciling equipment	18
Paints and materials	20
Applicators	22
Caring for tools	24

Types of stencils

There are three main types of stencils: single-layer, multiple-layer, and detailing. With single-layer stencils, the complete design, including any details, appears on one sheet. Multiple-layer stencils usually use a separate layer for each color in the stencil, and detailing stencils add intricate shapes to a simple stencil design. A single-layer stencil is the quickest to use. A multiple-layer stencil is the simplest to use but takes more time because each color is applied with a different stencil. A detailing stencil is the most complicated to design but produces the most sophisticated and elaborate results. Manufactured stencils are available in five materials; four of them also are available as sheets for designing and making your own stencils.

STENCIL TYPES

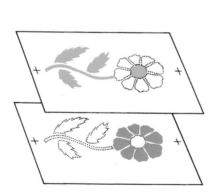
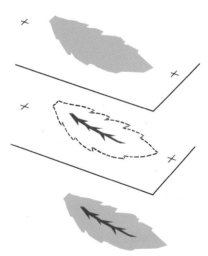

Single-layer stencils
All the colors are applied using one stencil. Although you have to be careful to use the correct colors and cutouts, the colors intermix for interesting effects. The bridges, or thin plastic divisons, are unique to this type. Most of the designs in this book use a single-layer stencil.

Multiple-layer stencils
A separate stencil is made for each color so the colors can't intermix. Multiple-layer stenciling is time-consuming, and the stencils need to be taped in place with care. The lack of color gradation, unless tones or highlights are added (see Step 4 on page 31), means the result can appear flat and stark.

Detailing stencils
A single-layer stencil is used for the main outlines, then details are added with one or more stencils using either different colors or a different intensity of the same color. Detailing stencils let you make more intricate shapes than would be possible with the other types of stencils.

MATERIALS FOR MAKING STENCILS

Clear acetate

A thin plastic sheet offering some of the advantages of transparent polyester, clear acetate also stretches. If you cut it into a sharp point, it may rip. It also becomes brittle with use. Use an acetate stencil only a few times.

Oiled stencil card

Together with brass, oiled stencil card is the traditional material for stencils. The card, which has been soaked in linseed oil, is fairly pliable and somewhat waterproof. It isn't transparent, so you have to transfer a design onto it rather than copying it directly onto the surface. However, it's fairly durable and easy to use.

Transparent polyester

This strong sheet material is transparent, so you can copy your design directly onto it and still see the surface beneath. It's easy to use and durable.

Drafting film

A cheaper form of tracing paper, drafting film is easy to cut. But it's not durable and is best used for small one-time designs.

Brass

Used for some manufactured stencils, brass is tough but difficult to use because it's so inflexible. If you bend it, it won't lie flat and will let colors bleed, making the stencil unusable.

COMPARING STENCIL MATERIALS

MATERIAL	COST	READILY AVAILABLE	DURABLE	CUTTING METHOD	ABLE TO BE CLEANED	FLEXIBLE	WATER-PROOF	NUMBER OF USES
Oiled card	Inexpensive	Yes	Fair	Crafts knife	No	No	Fairly	40–50 uses
Drafting film	Inexpensive	Yes	No	Crafts knife	No	Yes	Fairly	40–50 uses
Brass	Expensive	No	Yes	Precut	Yes	No	Yes	100+ uses
Transparent acetate	Inexpensive	Yes	Fair	Crafts knife Hot knife	Yes	Yes	Yes	100+ uses
Transparent polyester	Inexpensive	Yes	Yes	Crafts knife Hot knife	Yes	Yes	Yes	300+ uses

Stenciling equipment

For clear, sharp-edged results, a stencil must be securely attached to the surface to be decorated. It also must be easy to remove and reposition for further stenciling without marking or damaging the surface. Luckily, there are several supplies that will help you do just that. If you want to design and cut your own stencils, some special equipment will make the job much easier and more efficient. A number of common decorating materials to make your stenciling projects run smoother also will be helpful.

FOR ATTACHING A STENCIL TO A SURFACE

Masking tape
Attaches a stencil to a surface. Low-tack tape is the best, or detack it yourself (see Step 5 on page 29).

Repositioning spray adhesive
Applied to the back of a stencil to hold it securely in place. The stencil can be removed easily and reapplied elsewhere. Available from art stores and graphic supplies shops.

CAUTION
Always follow the manufacturer's instructions when using spray adhesive. To avoid inhaling the fumes, wear a mask and work in a well-ventilated area. Avoid contact with eyes or skin. Spray adhesive also is highly flammable: Keep it away from heat, don't smoke while using it, and dispose of empty aerosol cans safely. Store it well out of the reach of children.

FOR MAKING AND CUTTING STENCILS

Solvent-based permanent pen
Ink from this pen can't smudge, making it ideal for drawing a stencil design on transparent plastic materials (see pages 16–17).

Crafts knife
A slim-style crafts knife is best. Its sharp blade ensures accuracy and a smooth line, but it takes skill and control to use. Use with a resealable cutting mat. It's the best method for cutting card.

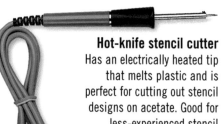

Hot-knife stencil cutter
Has an electrically heated tip that melts plastic and is perfect for cutting out stencil designs on acetate. Good for less-experienced stencil cutters because it's easy to use. Must be used with a glass base.

Plate glass
Designs to be cut with a hot-knife stencil cutter (left) should be placed over a sheet of plate glass before cutting. Either use polished-edge glass or bind cut edges with masking tape.

Cutting mat

A professional resealable cutting mat has a surface that reseals after running a knife across it, making it worth the expense. The surface also helps to restrain the knife, preventing overcuts.

Tracing paper

Necessary for transferring an original design onto stencil card. Because it's waterproof, it sometimes can be used to cut a stencil for a single use.

Correction tape

Special tape used to repair stencils because it's hard-wearing. Available at office supply stores.

OTHER USEFUL TOOLS AND MATERIALS

Stepladder

Essential for stenciling out-of-reach areas. When buying a stepladder, choose one that has a safety handle and platform for holding the palette while you work. When working high up on a wall, use two stepladders with a board between them.

SAFETY NOTE

Make sure your stepladder is secure and on an even surface before climbing it. Adjust the ladder as necessary.

Absorbent paper towels

Useful for removing excess paint from the brush.

Chalk

Marks design position. Choose a color you can see but that's not too different from the surface color. Wipe it off later with a damp cloth. Or, use a soft pencil and an eraser.

Steel rule

Measures from a straight edge to the position for a single stencil border.

Lining paper

Use as scrap paper to try out a stencil design, repeating it until you're satisfied; or to mask around a stencil when spray paint is applied (see page 29).

Palette or plate

Useful for holding and mixing colors. A sectioned disposable plate is ideal.

Scissors

Use small, sharp-pointed scissors to repair stencils, and larger scissors to cut sheets of transparent stencil material.

Cotton towel

Useful for drying damp brushes and for wiping up spilled paint.

Drop cloths

Drop cloths are useful for protecting the surfaces beneath an item being stenciled and to avoid overspray when using spray paints.

Level

Checks horizontal and vertical lines and ensures accurate stencil alignment.

Paints and materials

Water-based and oil-based paints can be used for stenciling, but some paints are better to use over specific bases than others (see the chart on pages 40–41). Also, some paints take a long time to dry—you'll work faster if you use acrylic, stencil, or spray paints, or stencil crayons. When using oil-based paints, clean tools and materials with the right solvent. For water-based paints, use water.

WATER-BASED PAINTS

Acrylics
Acrylic paints come in a wide range of colors at a reasonable cost. Because they can dry too quickly, they may an extender to prolong drying time. Available from art stores, acrylics also can be mixed to obtain custom colors.

Stencil paints
These fast-drying, high-pigment, water-based paints are specially designed for stenciling. Use strong colors but apply a minimum of paint. Colors can be mixed.

Fabric paints
Always use special fabric paints on fabrics that are going to be washed regularly. They're available at crafts stores.

Low-cost water-based
These paints are not the best for stenciling because their thinness often requires application of more than one coat and also may cause unsightly bleeding beneath the stencil.

CLEANING UP
Clear the sink area and use warm running water to wash all tools and materials. If the paint has dried, use a little detergent and soak the tools to soften the paint. Then wash as above. For an extra-clean brush, after you've washed out most of the paint, soak the brush for a few hours in a pail of water, then rinse again.

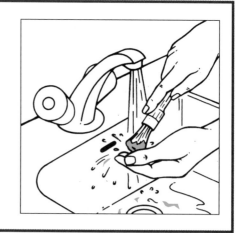

OIL-BASED PAINTS

Ceramic paints

Designed for use on ceramic or glass surfaces, ceramic paints also are ideal for stenciling onto tiles. Cold-cure ceramic paints are best because they don't require firing in an oven afterward.

Artist's oils

Oils come in a wide range of colors, but aren't ideal for stenciling because they take up to two days to dry. They're available at art stores.

Spray paints

Aerosol spray paints, found at most automotive supply stores, come in a wide range of colors and create a wonderfully subtle effect. However, they're not easy to use and require practice to get good results. See the caution below.

Stencil crayons

Sticks of solid oil-based paint can be found at some art supply stores. The crayon is rubbed onto a palette and the paint picked up with a brush (see pages 32–33). There's a wide range of colors available, and you also can mix colors. However, some shades fade with time.

Gloss, semigloss, and satin-finish oil-based paints

Manufactured in a wide range of colors, they need a long drying time and so are best used only for one-color stencils.

CAUTION

Always follow the manufacturer's instructions when using spray paints. Wear a mask and work in a well-ventilated area—outside, if possible. Avoid contact with eyes or skin. These paints also are highly flammable: Keep them away from heat, don't smoke while using them, and dispose of cans safely. Store well out of the reach of children.

VARNISHES

Water-based varnish

Ideal for protecting the finished work because it's clear and doesn't yellow with age the way oil-based varnish does. Apply it through the cutouts of a stencil or over the complete surface.

Oil-based varnish

Especially tough, oil-based varnish is best used for protecting stencils that have been painted onto furniture or floors. (see page 33).

Applicators

The only type of paint that doesn't require a separate applicator is aerosol spray paint. The most common applicator for stenciling is a special brush with short, chopped-off bristles. A brush produces the best shaded effects; a sponge will cover the surface more quickly and is ideal for large areas and for simulating natural materials like stone, moss, and grass. Whichever applicator you choose, use as little paint as possible, and go over the surface a number of times to build up color gradually, especially with deep colors and shading.

STENCIL BRUSHES

▶ **Soft, domed brushes**
Use with a swirling motion or a stippling action (see Stenciling Techniques on page 31). This brush creates a soft effect and is quick and easy to use. The domed end of the brush can be pinched to a point for fine-detail shading. One brush does most jobs, although you'll need a separate brush for each color you use.

▼ **Stiff, flat-topped brushes**
Use for stippling to give the results shown in Stenciling Techniques on page 31. Stippling is hard work and you'll be tempted to speed the job by applying too much paint at once. Too much paint, however, results in a blot on the wall (see pages 36–37). These brushes aren't easy to control. You will need smaller brushes for shading.

MAKE YOUR OWN STENCIL BRUSH
If you can't find a stencil brush, a standard paintbrush bound with masking tape is a good substitute. Use a small brush, less than 2 inches wide, and bind it about 1 inch from the ends of the bristles.

SPONGES

Both natural and synthetic sponges will work. A sponge is ideal for applying color to large areas such as a floor or mock-stone pillar. The paint should be slightly diluted so the sponge doesn't become clogged. However, you must be careful not to overload the sponge or bleeding will occur. Remove excess paint before you start (see page 35).

SPRAYERS

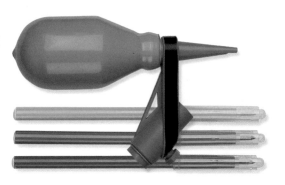

▼ **Natural sea sponge**
This produces a soft, broken finish that's especially effective in creating depth and texture when different colors are sponged on simultaneously.

Air marker and aerosol spray

The stippled effect produced by these applicators is attractive. You'll need to practice both methods though. The air marker uses air to blow the paint from the end of the felt tip, through the stencil, and onto the surface. Be especially careful to apply the paint evenly. For safe use of aerosol spray paints, see page 21.

◀ **Synthetic sponge**
Colors can be wiped over the surface or dabbed on with a synthetic sponge.

THE EFFECTS OF DIFFERENT APPLICATORS

Stiff brush

Soft brush

Sponge

Air marker

Aerosol spray

Caring for tools

Taking proper care of your tools pays dividends. Wash brushes immediately after use, and clean stencils regularly to avoid clogging and ensure crisp outlines. Narrow bridges between adjacent cutouts in stencils can break during use or cleaning, so clean stencils with care. If they do break, they're easy to fix. Just do it right away so they don't put extra pressure on the delicate surface while the stencil is in use.

Cleaning and storing brushes
TOOLS: Brush to be cleaned, hair dryer
MATERIALS: Water or solvent, towel, paper towels, rubber bands or string

Cleaning a stencil
TOOLS: Stencil to be cleaned, nylon abrasive kitchen pad
MATERIALS: Water or solvent, spray adhesive solvent, absorbent paper towels, sheets of plastic

Repairing a stencil
TOOLS: Torn stencil, scissors or crafts knife
MATERIALS: Correction tape

CLEANING AND STORING BRUSHES

1 Immediately after finishing work, clean the brushes used with water-based paint by rinsing them under warm, running water. Clean brushes used with oil-based paint with the appropriate solvent. Then towel-dry all brushes completely.

2 Bind a strip of paper towel around the bristles to keep them straight, and hold it in place with a rubber band or piece of string. Let the brush dry in a warm place, then store it flat so the bristles will keep their original shape.

TO REUSE A BRUSH IMMEDIATELY

After washing, towel-dry the brush, then finish the drying process with a hair dryer. After final use, clean as before, and store the brush with the bristles bound as shown at left.

CLEANING A STENCIL

1 Stencils need regular cleaning. If water-based paint has dried, first soak the stencil in warm water to soften the paint. Lay the stencil on a flat surface and rub gently with a damp nylon abrasive pad; finally, rinse. Clean off oil-based paint with the appropriate solvent as soon as possible.

2 The spray adhesive on the back may be removed with a solvent recommended by the manufacturer or with nail-polish remover. Or, try using a liquid detergent solution and carefully scrub with a nylon abrasive pad as in Step 1.

3 Dry the cleaned stencil with absorbent paper towels, then store it flat between two sheets of thick plastic.

BEFORE MAKING REPAIRS

Always clean a stencil before repairing it (spray paint is almost impossible to remove, but there is little buildup so you can leave whatever remains). If a stencil tears while you're working with it, reapply spray adhesive to the back, attempting to keep the pieces together until you finish the job. Don't try this if you've just begun to stencil a repeated design over a large area. Instead, repair the stencil as shown at right.

REPAIRING A TORN STENCIL

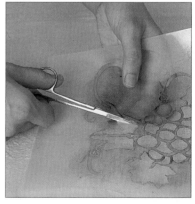

1 Breaks in a stencil are repaired with correction tape (see page 19). Apply a short length of tape to each side of the stencil across the tear to hold it securely in place.

2 Carefully cut away the excess tape with a small pair of scissors to leave the stencil design as it was before the damage. Or, use a crafts knife to remove the excess tape.

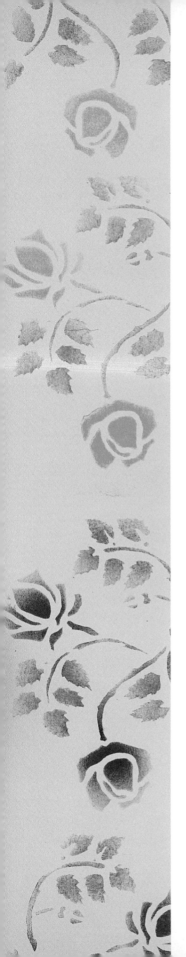

Basic Techniques

Stenciling is an easily mastered skill that anyone can learn with a little know-how. Once you learn the basic techniques—marking and attaching a stencil, applying paint, and protecting the finished design—you're free to create your own designs and special effects. Remember to use a damp cloth to remove any chalk marks you made when positioning the stencils. And when stenciling onto a dark background, apply white stencil paint first.

Two people can start with the same stencil design and the same color scheme but produce totally different results. So, even though stenciling isn't difficult, the finished effect still can be unique. Don't be afraid to make mistakes; most are simple to fix. And if you simply take some time at the start to experiment on scrap paper and perfect your colors and stenciling techniques, most mistakes won't even occur in the first place.

This chapter contains

Positioning stencils	28
Using stencil paints	30
Using stencil crayons	32
Stenciling large areas	34
Correcting mistakes	36

Positioning stencils

Before starting to stencil, check that the surface to be painted is in good overall condition. You also need to carefully work out where the design will go. On a large area, such as a wall or floor, take measurements and draw chalk lines to pinpoint positions. When you've done this, attach the stencil at the first point to be decorated. To avoid seepage, the stencil will have to fit tightly against the object to be stenciled. But when you're done painting, you'll need to remove it without damaging the base surface.

TOOLS: Chalk, metal rule, level, stencil

MATERIALS: Repositioning spray adhesive,* masking tape, lining paper or newspaper, solvent

*For safe use of spray adhesive, see page 18.

1 Make sure that the surface to be decorated is sound and that no damage will result when the stencil is removed. Make a test sample on a similar surface to determine which stenciling technique will work best (see charts, pages 40–41).

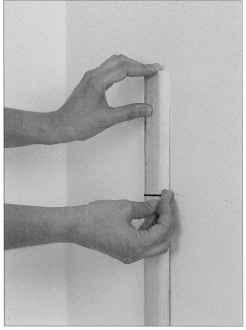

2 Work out the exact positions for the stencils. To do this, use chalk to mark points that line up with the stencil edges not the center of the design.

3 For a border design, measure from the nearest parallel surface—the ceiling, baseboard, or chair rail—and mark at about 12-inch intervals along the wall. Use a level to be sure the marks you have made are level.

4 Place the stencil on newspaper or paper with the side to be painted facedown. Hold the can about 8 to 12 inches away from the surface and spray a mist of adhesive to cover the entire stencil back. Use solvent to remove excess adhesive, if necessary.

5 Detack the masking tape to be used by repeatedly sticking the tape onto a piece of fabric until you can see tiny fibers on the back and it feels less sticky. Apply the stencil to the surface to be decorated. Add short strips of masking tape to the edges, if necessary. Make sure the stencil is straight and is attached securely. Stand back to check it visually, then rub your hand over the surface to make sure it adheres well. After use, remove the tape as soon as possible.

UNBLOCKING A SPRAY NOZZLE

If the nozzle on the can of adhesive spray becomes blocked, remove it and soak for at least 10 minutes in the solvent recommended by the manufacturer, or use nail-polish remover. Rub off any excess adhesive, then use a pin to clean out the nozzle. Point the nozzle away from your eyes.

MASKING THE STENCIL

When using spray paint, you'll need to protect a wide area surrounding the stencil to avoid overspray. Mask an area of at least 12 inches on all sides of the stencil, using lining paper held in place with masking tape.

Using stencil paints

Once the stencil is in position, you're ready to begin. Load the brush sparingly with paint and use one of the two main stenciling techniques—swirling or stippling—to apply it. Swirling creates a smooth, soft effect, and stippling produces a dotted, textured finish.

    You can combine the two techniques or use just one of them to highlight texture. Apply the paint in extremely thin layers using an almost-dry brush, and the finish will soon acquire the cloudy, translucent quality that's the hallmark of fine stenciling.

TOOLS: Stencil, stencil brushes

MATERIALS: Water-based stencil paints, palette (or old plate), scrap paper, newspaper

1 Assemble all of your tools and materials. Shake the paint so the inner lid is well coated, and pour some paint from the lid onto the palette. Work with 1 teaspoon at a time.

2 Dip the tip of the brush into paint without overloading it, removing the excess on a scrap of paper. Using too much paint causes the paint to bleed under the stencil edges and creates a heavy-looking finish.

3 Work the paint into the bristles. To do this, swirl the paint on the brush onto a clean part of the palette. Do this between 5 and 30 times until the brush feels tacky and nearly dry.

STENCILING TECHNIQUES

A circular, swift swirling action of the hand and brush gives a smooth effect that you'll find quick to produce.

For a stippled effect, use a tapping motion, dabbing evenly up and down all over the surface.

4 Use either a circular or a stippling motion to apply paint. To build up color where you want it, simply apply more layers of paint. To shade a design, observe how light falls on natural objects or study tonal drawings. Use darker tones for areas in shade and white or a paler shade of the original color for highlights.

5 Once the design is complete, remove the stencil to inspect your work. If you missed an area or some part needs extra shading, carefully replace the stencil to complete it.

TEST BEFORE YOU START

It's very important to make a test sample before stenciling the actual surface. A length of lining paper makes a good sample sheet. Use it to perfect your technique, then live with the sample for a few days so you can see it in both natural and artificial light. Adjust the coloring if necessary. Once you're satisfied with the result, you're ready to start.

Using stencil crayons

As an alternative to water-based paints, you can use oil-based stencil crayons. These are solid sticks that, when rubbed onto a hard surface, soften so you can pick up the paint with a brush and treat it just like other paints.

The advantage of using stencil crayons is that they make it almost impossible to load too much paint onto the brush. The tough finish of oil-based paint makes stencil crayons ideal for use on shiny surfaces like tiles, as well as surfaces that already have been painted with oil-based paint.

When your stencil is completed in an area that will receive hard wear, such as on a floor or a piece of furniture, coat your design with varnish to protect it.

*For safe use of spray adhesive, see page 18.

Using stencil crayons
TOOLS: Stencils, stencil brushes
MATERIALS: Spray adhesive,* masking tape, oil-based stencil crayons, palette

Protecting the work
TOOLS: Stencil, household paintbrush or stencil brush
MATERIALS: Spray adhesive, masking tape, water- or oil-based varnish

STENCIL-CRAYON TECHNIQUE

1 Apply spray adhesive to the stencil back, then position it and add masking tape (see pages 28–29). Remove the dry tip of the stencil crayon by rubbing it on scrap paper. Rub the crayon on the palette. The creamy paint left behind is ready to use.

2 Load up the brush with paint by working the brush over the palette in a swirling motion. Check that the paint is evenly distributed on the brush so your stencil will appear evenly painted.

3 Use the swirling technique to produce a smooth, blended effect. If you add new colors to the same area later, they'll blend to produce a totally new overall color.

COLOR FADING
Unless you'd like some colors in your design to fade, avoid dark greens and dark reds when using stencil crayons. These shades easily fade when exposed to light, moisture, and steam.

4 The use of stencil crayons produces an even finish. Colors blend rather than remaining separate, making for less shading than with other methods. Building up color is difficult because you have to wait for the paint to dry between layers; it takes hours to partially set and days to dry to its final hardness.

PROTECTING YOUR WORK

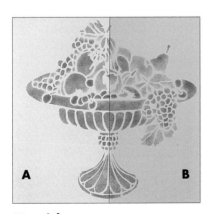

Varnish
Water-based varnish (A) is clear and easy to apply. Use it over water-based paints such as acrylics. Polyurethane varnish (B) yellows with age. Use it over oil-based paints (gloss, eggshell, satin-finish).

Small areas
If just the stencil design needs protection, or if the surface around the design can't be varnished, apply the varnish by brushing it through the cutout spaces of the stencil.

The complete surface
Better protection is provided if the whole surface is varnished. Apply a thin coat of varnish for light protection, two or three coats for a tough finish. Allow each coat to dry thoroughly.

Stenciling large areas

Sponging with a sea sponge or synthetic sponge and spraying with aerosol spray paints are the quickest ways to apply paint to large areas.

When sponging, the paint will have to be slightly diluted and the sponge applied almost dry or bleeding can occur, leaving smudged outlines. When using the spray method, be sure to protect a wide area surrounding the stencil to avoid overspray. Spraying will take practice to get the light, even results you want. Make samples on scrap paper to perfect your technique before you start work on the actual surface to be stenciled.

*For safe use of spray adhesive and aerosol spray paint, see pages 18 and 21.

Spray painting
TOOLS: Stencil
MATERIALS: Spray adhesive,* masking tape, aerosol spray paints,* lining paper, drop cloths

Stenciling with a sponge
TOOLS: Stencil, natural sea sponge
MATERIALS: Stencil paint, spray adhesive,* masking tape, glass jar, plate

STENCILING WITH SPRAY PAINT

1 Position the stencil and protect the area around it with a mask (see pages 28–29). Start to spray from the edges of the stencil, then continue across using a light touch and moving the can the whole time.

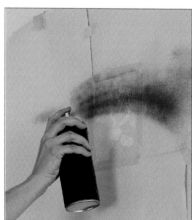

2 Apply light subsequent layers of paint in the same way where you want to build up color. Use either the same color or new colors. As many as ten coats may be needed for good coverage of any one area.

3 To add highlights, use yellow spray paint; to shade areas, use a dark tone. Apply highlights and tones where light and shade would naturally fall (see Step 4 on page 31).

STENCILING WITH A SPONGE

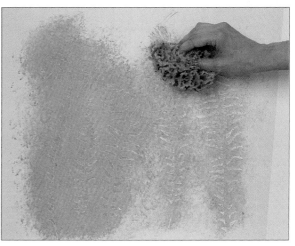

1 Attach the stencil (see pages 28–29). Dilute the paint with water in the glass jar. For strong colors, use about 8 ounces of water to 1 tablespoon of paint. Work the paint into the sponge and remove any excess before you start stenciling.

2 Use a gentle dabbing motion to apply the paint to the surface. Join the sponged shapes to form an overall, densely mottled effect.

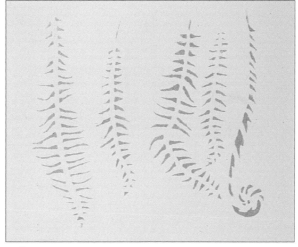

3 Use the second color more lightly so the first color still shows through. This second coat adds texture and depth. Extra colors can be added but aren't usually necessary.

4 The finished stencil shows the texture produced by the sponge. Use this method to reproduce natural materials such as plants, sand, soil, grass, and stone.

ATTACHING LARGE STENCILS

Large, heavy stencils may need masking tape as well as spray adhesive to hold them securely in place.

Apply the tape in short strips at each corner and add extra strips at the top of the stencil if necessary. Remember to detack the masking tape and to remove it as soon as possible or you may ruin your base surface (see Step 5 on page 29).

Correcting mistakes

Everyone makes mistakes from time to time, but luckily most mistakes occur at the practice stage. Always make test samples on scrap paper to iron out any problems before you start work on the actual surface to be stenciled. The most likely times for mistakes to happen are when you position the stencil and when you apply the paint. Make sure the stencil is securely attached and accurately positioned, and apply the minimum amount of paint with a soft brush.

MISTAKES: HOW TO PREVENT AND CORRECT THEM

PROBLEM	CAUSE	PREVENTION	SOLUTION
Paint seepage	Too much paint	Use less paint Use spray adhesive	Dry stencil, paint out mistake
Stenciling too faint	Too little paint Paint color similar to base	Use more paint, or darker color Always test a sample first	Replace stencil and redo
Design not straight	Chalk line not used or stencil itself was not cut straight	Level should be used to check horizontals and verticals Check stencil and recut edges	Paint out crooked section and redo
Incorrect color	Wrong color on the brush	Check the color on the brush	Replace stencil, use white or base color to stencil it out, then redo in correct color
Color too strong	Too much paint used Color of stencil paint too strong	Check colors against base before use Always test a sample first	Replace stencil, use white or base color to stencil it out, then redo in correct color
Second overlay incorrectly positioned	Stencil guidelines are incorrect Poorly positioned	Test a sample before starting	Paint out the stencil and redo
A background color or pattern shows through	Surface stenciling doesn't cover the base color or pattern	Stencil in white first. Allow to dry and restencil in the correct colors	Replace stencil, stencil in white and allow to dry, restencil in correct colors
Blurred edges	No spray adhesive used	Use spray adhesive	Paint out area and redo

AVOIDING THE MOST COMMON MISTAKES

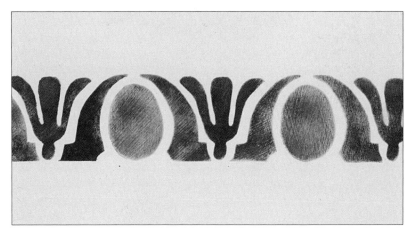

1 Using a chalk line as a guide to position a stencil makes sure that it will be straight. A crooked design usually is the result of inadequate preparation in planning exactly where the design should go. Always follow the same procedure for positioning and attaching stencils (see pages 28–29).

2 The crooked stencil job shown here can't be fixed. To start over, paint this section out, draw in the guideline, and repaint. Curling floral designs that are crooked sometimes can be disguised by repositioning the stencil to add extra sections of the design at strategic points to help balance the overall appearance.

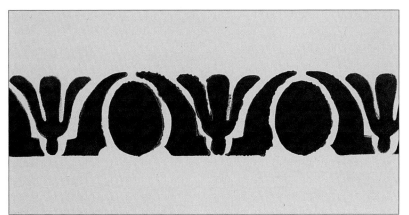

3 Paint seepage usually occurs when a brush contains too much paint. Make sure the brush is almost dry when you start— check it on scrap paper first. Always reposition the stencil with spray adhesive to reduce the chance of seepage.

GETTING IT RIGHT

If you're confident yet careful, you're more likely to have stenciling success. But even if you make a mistake, go ahead and finish the job. Then stand back and see if the mistake is noticeable. If you decide the mistake needs correcting, remedy it by following the information in the chart on page 36, Mistakes: How to Prevent and Correct Them.

Surfaces to Stencil

Stenciled designs can be applied to most surfaces and are commonly used on walls, floors, furniture, fabrics, and tiles. However, the paint you use must be compatible with the surface, and in hard-wear areas, protected so it doesn't wear off. On most fabrics, a washable fabric paint is best. On ceramics, tiles, and glass, use a ceramic paint.

Rough-textured surfaces are best stenciled using a stippling motion instead of a swirling action to apply the paint. Some surfaces, such as terra-cotta and bare wood, can be stenciled with ordinary water-based stencil paints—but varnish them for protection.

This chapter contains

Base surfaces	40
Walls	42
Wall surfaces	44
Doors	45
Paneling a flush door	46
Floors	48
Furniture	50
Fabrics	52
Fabric paints	54
Stenciled fabrics	55
Tiles	56

Base surfaces

Although most paints will adhere to most surfaces, some are more suitable for stenciling than others. These charts show the best paints for a variety of base surfaces, the best methods to apply them, the type of stencil to use, how to attach it, and the best varnish to protect the finished design.

BASE SURFACES—PAINTS

BASE SURFACE	WATER-BASED STENCIL	WATER-BASED	ACRYLIC	FABRIC	ARTIST'S OIL	CERAMIC	SATIN FINISH	SPRAY	CRAYON
Water-based	•	•	•	•	•		•	•	•
Satin finish	•	•	•		•		•	•	•
Gloss					•		•	•	
Varnished bare wood	•	•	•	•	•		•	•	
Sealed wood	•	•	•		•		•	•	
Melamine	•	•	•		•		•	•	•
Cotton	•	•	•	•			•	•	•
Silk	•	•	•	•				•	•
Glass						•		•	
Ceramic/china						•		•	•
Tiles (gloss)						•		•	•
Tiles (matte)						•		•	•
Acrylic plastic	•	•	•		•		•	•	•
Terra-cotta	•	•	•		•		•	•	•
Textured wallpaper	•	•	•	•	•		•	•	•
Expanded vinyl	•	•	•	•	•		•	•	•
Wood-chip (rare in U.S.)		•	•	•	•		•	•	•
Bricks	•	•	•	•	•		•	•	•
Grass	•	•	•					•	
Tongue-and-groove panel	•	•	•	•	•		•	•	•
Cakes	*Use edible food coloring*								

BASE SURFACES—METHODS

BASE SURFACE	STENCIL RESTRICTIONS	HOW TO ATTACH STENCIL	APPLICATION METHOD	PROTECTION
Water-based	None	Spray adhesive, masking tape	Brush/spray/sponge	Water-based varnish
Satin finish	None	Spray adhesive, masking tape	Brush/spray/sponge	Oil-based varnish
Gloss	None	Spray adhesive, masking tape	Brush/spray/sponge	Oil-based varnish
Varnished bare wood	None	Spray adhesive, masking tape	Brush/spray/sponge	Any varnish
Sealed wood	None	Spray adhesive, masking tape	Brush/spray/sponge	Any varnish
Melamine	None	Spray adhesive, masking tape	Brush/spray/sponge	Water-based varnish
Cotton	None	Spray adhesive, masking tape	Brush/spray/sponge	Iron to set
Silk	None	Spray adhesive, masking tape	Brush	Set as instructed
Glass	None	Spray adhesive, masking tape	Brush/spray	Set as instructed
Ceramic/china	None	Spray adhesive, masking tape	Brush/spray	Set as instructed
Tiles (gloss)	None	Spray adhesive, masking tape	Brush/spray	Set as instructed
Tiles (matte)	None	Spray adhesive, masking tape	Brush/spray	Set as instructed
Acrylic plastic	None	Spray adhesive, masking tape	Brush/spray	Water-based varnish
Terra-cotta	None	Spray adhesive, masking tape	Brush/spray/sponge	Water-based varnish
Textured wallpaper	Large stencil, simple design	Spray adhesive, masking tape	Brush/spray	Water-based varnish
Expanded vinyl	Large stencil, simple design	Spray adhesive, masking tape	Brush/spray/sponge	Water-based varnish
Wood-chip (rare in U.S.)	Large stencil, simple design	Spray adhesive, masking tape	Brush/spray/sponge	Water-based varnish
Bricks	Large stencil, simple design	Spray adhesive, masking tape	Brush/spray	Water-based varnish
Grass	Large stencil, simple design	Spray adhesive, masking tape	Brush/spray/sponge	None
Tongue-and-groove panel	None	Spray adhesive, masking tape	Brush/spray	Water-based varnish
Cakes	None	Sugar solution	Brush	None

Walls

When decorating walls, consider the style and use of the room. Take into account fabrics, carpets, wall texture, the style of the house, and the atmosphere you want to create. Are you looking for a slick, formal effect or a country-cottage look? The style of the stencil and the colors you use should take these factors into account. Stencils can be applied to walls as a border design (see below), as a frieze (see pages 60–61), as a grouped arrangement (see pages 62–63), or as a complete wall treatment (see pages 80–81).

*For safe use of spray adhesive, see page 18.

TOOLS: Steel rule, level, chalk, stencil, stencil brushes

MATERIALS: Spray adhesive,* masking tape, water-based paint, palette

USING A WALL BORDER

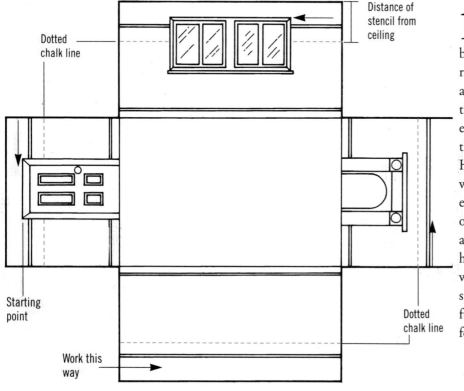

Dotted chalk line

Distance of stencil from ceiling

Starting point

Dotted chalk line

Work this way

1 First decide on the position for your border. Used at chair-rail or picture-rail level, a border will lower the ceiling, working especially well in a room that has a high ceiling. However, in a room with a low ceiling, this effect could be overpowering. Borders also can be used to highlight a decorative window, show off a special piece of furniture, or edge a focal-point doorway.

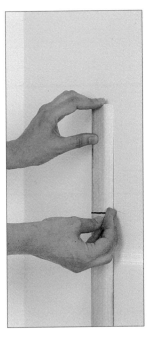

2 When you've decided on the position, make chalk guide marks along the wall. Mark the position and prepare the stencil (see pages 28–29). Attach the stencil for the first application of paint in an out-of-the-way spot—above a door, in an alcove, or behind a large piece of furniture. Then you can perfect your technique mostly out of view. Apply paint to the stencil (see pages 30–35).

3 As you move along the wall, line up each stencil with your chalk marks. At a corner, gently tap the stencil into place on the wall you're working on, keeping the section on the other wall free. Stencil up to the corner, then position the remaining section of stencil on the adjacent wall, peeling away the section you just completed.

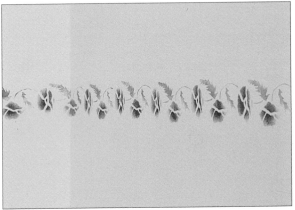

4 Because of your preparation work, each section of the stencil will line up with the rest. Remove any remaining chalk marks with a damp cloth.

LOCATING A BORDER

When using a narrow border, consider running it around both the top and bottom edges of the wall. You also can use a border to edge the ceiling, much the way a plaster frieze often edges the ceilings in older homes.

TO MITER A CORNER

On a border that surrounds a window or embellishes a floor or piece of furniture, miter the corners. Start stenciling at a corner. Draw a chalk line diagonally across the stencil design to create a miter, then mask all cutout shapes beyond the drawn line. Stencil one side of the corner, then flip the stencil over to paint the adjacent corner section. Repeat this procedure on each of the other corners.

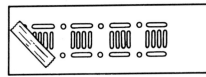

Mask the stencil at a corner, then flip it to turn the corner and produce the result shown at left.

Wall surfaces

Some stenciling techniques are best for specific wall surfaces. Similarly, rough or uneven wall surfaces will cry out for simple, bold stencil designs. The chart below lists a variety of wall textures and suggests the best stenciling method and stencil type to use with each.

STENCILING TECHNIQUES

SURFACE	STENCILING METHOD	TYPE OF STENCIL
Flat wall	Stipple, swirl, or spray	Any
Textured wallpaper	Stipple or spray	Larger, simple designs
Tongue-and-groove paneling	Stipple or swirl	Larger, simple designs
Concrete or brick	Stipple or spray	Larger, simple designs
Textured wall	Stipple or spray	Larger, simple designs
Terra-cotta	Stipple, swirl, or spray	Any

Stenciling on brick

Textured wallpaper

Textured wall

Doors

Doors get more wear and tear than almost any other surface. Using oil-based paint will ensure that they're easy to clean and touch up. To stencil over an oil-based paint surface, always use a compatible, durable paint. Paints such as satin-finish oil-based, semigloss, and gloss are compatible, as is aerosol automotive spray paint. (For information on using spray paint, see page 34.)

Stenciling significantly changes the look of a door, enhancing a paneled door or creating the effect of panels on an ordinary flush door (see pages 46–47).

*For safe use of spray adhesive, see page 18.

Using oil-based paint
TOOLS: Stencil, stencil brushes

MATERIALS: Satin-finish oil-based paint, spray adhesive,* palette

USING OIL-BASED PAINT

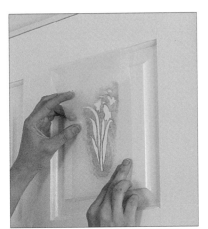

1 Spray the back of the stencil with adhesive and carefully position the stencil on the door (see page 29).

2 Apply satin-finish oil-based paint with a brush (see Steps 2–3 on pages 32–33). Because so little paint is used, it will dry in less than an hour. If you need to reposition the stencil close to a wet area, wait until the first area is dry.

BRUSHED PAINT VS. SPRAY PAINT

This comparison shows that, aside from the colors used, there's little difference in the results. Using satin-finish paint on a small area will take less time because no masking is needed.

Paneling a flush door

You can create a decidedly different-looking door using a stencil design that creates the effect of panels. Then you can embellish your panels with motifs such as flowers, figures, symbols, and animals to complement the room and its use. Adding shading and highlights (see Step 4 on page 31) will make the paneling even more realistic.

Or, add wooden bead molding and stencil inside and around it. If you use water-based paints for stenciling (see pages 40–41), applying two or three coats of varnish will give you a tougher finish (see page 33).

*For safe use of spray adhesive and aerosol spray paints, see pages 18 and 21.

Paneling a flush door
TOOLS: Stencil, stencil brushes

MATERIALS: Spray adhesive,* oil-based stencil crayons, palette

---

APPLYING A REPEAT PATTERN TO CREATE A CENTER PANEL

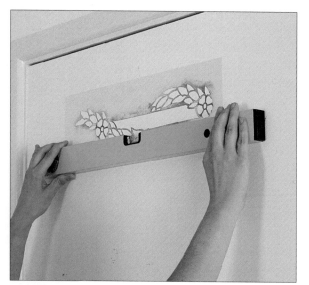

1 Measure the door and choose a stencil design that will create the effect of panels. Mark the stencil positions accurately, and check the first position with a level.

2 Spray the adhesive over the back of the stencil and position it carefully on the door (see pages 28–29). Use the brush to apply the paint to the stencil (see pages 32–33).

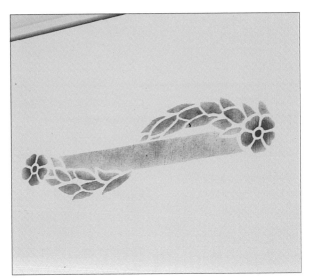

4 The design used here creates the effect of a center panel. If you decide to divide the door into smaller panels, choose a smaller design. Other ideas are shown in the "Ideas and Choices" chapter.

3 Remove the stencil and check your work. When you're happy with the results, reposition the stencil and complete the panel. Miter the corners if necessary (see page 43).

PANELING IDEAS

Beaded border ▶
Here, wood beading, available already mitered, was nailed to a flush door to create panels. The stenciled star and moon create a focal point for each of the panels.

Painted border ▶
A painted border stripe creates a paneled edge to frame a centered stencil design. To make straight lines when you're painting stripes, stick strips of detacked masking tape along each side of the stripe. Remove it as soon as you're done painting, before the paint dries.

Floors

A wood floor provides an ideal surface for stenciling and, when protected by several coats of varnish, is hard wearing and easy to clean. When planning a design, keep in mind the location of furniture, and always draw out your design first. Design ideas include a border, a striped or checkerboard design, a painted rug with tassels, stenciled shadows to give the impression of perpetual sunshine, and giant paw prints meandering through the room. Match the patterns used on walls or furniture for a coordinated effect, or use different motifs that incorporate the same theme.

Floor border
TOOLS: Stencils, stencil brushes, steel rule

MATERIALS: Spray adhesive, masking tape, water-based stencil paint, palette, water-based floor varnish

Checkerboard floor design
TOOLS: Fine-grit sandpaper, stencils, sponge

MATERIALS: Water-based varnish, straightedge, chalk, spray adhesive,* masking tape, water-based stencil paints, plate, floor-grade polyurethane varnish

*For safe use of spray adhesive, see page 18.

FLOOR BORDER

1 Work on a newly sanded floor if you can. Then, apply a coat of water-based varnish to protect the surface. If the floor is already varnished or polished, clean the surface with detergent, allow it to dry, and lightly sand it. Liberally spray the backs of the stencils with adhesive so they'll be kept in close contact with the floor, and arrange them carefully. Press them down firmly.

2 Apply the paint (see pages 30–31). Use a nearly dry brush and build up the paint in thin layers. Don't completely cover the grain of the wood; allow some of it to show through the paint.

3 When stenciling is complete, allow the last paint color to dry and brush on three coats of water-based, floor-grade varnish. Remember to let the first coat of varnish dry thoroughly before applying any subsequent coats.

CHECKERED FLOOR DESIGN

1 Prepare the floor as shown in Step 1, opposite. Work out the floor design, and draw the outline on the floor before you begin, using a straightedge and chalk. Then attach the stencil in the first position using spray adhesive.

2 Dilute the paint with equal parts of paint and water and work it into the sponge. Then apply the paint in a dabbing motion (see Steps 1–2 on page 35). Extra coats will give a denser finish, but the effect looks best if a little wood grain shows through the design.

3 When you've finished all of the stenciling, give the floor at least three coats of floor-grade varnish. It's best to maintain the surface by recoating it with varnish every six months or so.

Furniture

Stenciling will add interest and color to natural wood furniture. You even can disguise a poor surface by first painting it to match other furnishings in the room. However, large pieces of furniture lose impact if you paint them to match walls. Try to reflect the room scheme, possibly coordinating your stencil pattern with a design on your fabric window treatments or other fabrics in the room.

Child's toy box
TOOLS: Fine-grit sandpaper, synthetic sponge, 2-part stencils, household paintbrush, fine-grade steel wool

MATERIALS: Water-based stencil paint, spray adhesive, masking tape, palette, water-based varnish, wax polish

Melamine cupboard
TOOLS: Fine-grit sandpaper, stencils, household paintbrush

MATERIALS: Water-based or oil-based paint to match cupboard, spray adhesive,* masking tape, water-based stencil paint, palette, water-based varnish

*For safe use of spray adhesive, see page 18.

CHILD'S TOY BOX

1 Before color-washing natural wood, sand the surface to provide tooth. Make up the color wash with stencil paint (thin 1 part stencil paint to 5–10 parts water). Before applying the paint, test the color in an inconspicuous area. Add more water or paint if necessary, then apply with a sponge.

2 When the wash is dry, spray the adhesive on the back of the stencil and position it (see pages 28–29). Apply the paint (see pages 30–31). Some paint will be absorbed by the wood, letting the grain show through.

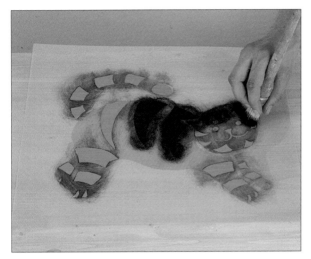

3 When the stencil for the box top is completed in the first color and is dry, remove the stencil, attach the second stencil, and apply the next color through the cutout shapes in this stencil. Continue until all of the colors are complete.

4 When the stenciling is finished and dry, brush on two coats of water-based varnish. Finally, add a little furniture wax applied with fine-grade steel wool, then buff with a soft, lint-free cloth.

MELAMINE CUPBOARD

1 If the surface is poor, first apply a coat of water- or oil-based paint to match the original color. To clean a surface in good condition, wipe it with a cloth wrung out in a solution of dishwashing liquid.

2 Work out the position for the design, mark the stencil positions, and attach the stencil (see pages 28–29). Mix the paint and apply it using the stippling technique (see Stenciling Techniques, page 31). Build up the color with additional applications.

3 When the stencil design is complete and dry, varnish the design area only. To do this, reposition the stencil carefully and apply water-based varnish through the stencil cutouts (see Protecting Your Work, page 33).

Fabrics

Natural fibers, such as cotton and linen, or a cotton-and-polyester blend are the best fabrics on which to stencil. Although fabric can be stenciled with almost any type of paint, if you're going to wash it often, it's best to use fabric paint that you set with a hot iron.

Fabric absorbs paint in a way that walls and painted furniture don't, so colors applied to fabrics usually appear softer. Before decorating it, wash the fabric to remove any sizing, and iron it well. It's also important to make a test sample to see how the colors will appear and to make sure they won't bleed. When you're satisfied with the colors and are sure they won't run, you're ready to start the actual fabric stenciling.

TOOLS: Stencil, pins, soft-bristled stencil brushes

MATERIALS: Fabric, protective plastic sheet, masking tape, spray adhesive,* water-based stencil or fabric paints, palette

*For safe use of spray adhesive, see page 18.

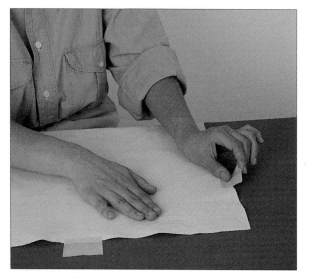

1 On a smooth surface, lay out the clean, dry, ironed fabric on top of a sheet of plastic—a plastic-coated tabletop is best. Using masking tape, tape a small piece of fabric to the table to hold it in place. Large pieces of heavy fabric need to be weighted down to keep them from slipping.

2 Use pins or dressmaker's chalk to mark the positions for the stencil on the fabric.

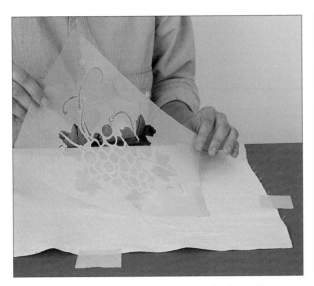

3 Spray the back of the stencil with the adhesive (see pages 28–29), and carefully lay the stencil in position, following the marked guidelines and making sure the fabric is flat. Remove and reposition it if necessary; creases cause an irregular color in the painted design.

4 A soft-bristled brush is essential here because it will work the paint into the fibers. A domed brush is useful for delicate shading. Pour out the paint, dip in the brush, and work the paint into the bristles (see Steps 2 and 3 on pages 30–31).

5 Apply the paint with either a swirling or stippling motion (see Stenciling Techniques, page 31). When the stencil is removed, you'll find that a tightly woven fabric produces clearer colors, and an open-weave fabric gives a more hazy effect. If you're using fabric paint, follow ironing instructions.

USING TOO MUCH PAINT
When stenciling clothing or commercial furnishings, always protect the fabric underneath the area you're working on to avoid color bleeding. And don't overload the brush with paint because this, too, can cause bleeding (see pages 36–37).

Fabric paints

Choose your paint based on the fabric to be stenciled and how it should be washed. Use the chart below to pick the appropriate paint for your chosen fabric or soft furnishing. The photographs opposite show you how the dried paint will appear on various fabrics.

FABRICS, PAINTS, AND CARE INSTRUCTIONS

FABRIC	PAINT	CARE Fabric paint	CARE Stencil paint	CARE Oil-based paint/spray
Cotton or polyester- and-cotton blends				
Tablecloth	Fabric paint	Iron to set Machine-wash Lasts as long as fabric		
Bed linen	Fabric, water-based stencil paint, satin-finish oil-based paint	Iron to set Machine-wash Lasts as long as fabric	Hand-wash 15–20 washes before fading	Hand-wash 50–100 washes before fading
Curtains	Fabric, water-based stencil paint, satin-finish oil-based paint	Iron to set Machine-wash Lasts as long as fabric	Hand-wash 15–20 washes before fading	Hand-wash 50–100 washes before fading
Cushion covers	Fabric, water-based stencil paint, satin-finish oil-based paint	Iron to set Machine-wash Lasts as long as fabric	Hand-wash 15–20 washes before fading	Hand-wash 50–100 washes before fading
Muslin	Fabric, water-based stencil paint, satin-finish oil-based paint	Iron to set Machine-wash Lasts as long as fabric	Hand-wash 15–20 washes before fading	Hand-wash 50–100 washes before fading
Silk	Silk paints are best	Set as recommended Hand-wash		
T-shirt material	Fabric, water-based stencil paint, satin-finish oil-based paint	Iron to set Machine-wash Lasts as long as fabric	Hand-wash 15–20 washes before fading	Hand-wash 50–100 washes before fading
Lampshades Cotton	Fabric, water-based stencil paint, satin-finish oil-based paint	Sponge clean with detergent solution when necessary	Sponge clean with detergent solution when necessary	Sponge clean with detergent solution when necessary
Cardboard	Water-based stencil paint, oil crayons, satin-finish oil-based paint, sprays		Dust as required	Dust as required
Roller blind	Water-based stencil paint, oil crayons, satin-finish oil-based paint, sprays		Dust as required	Dust as required
Shower curtain	Water-based stencil paint, oil crayons, satin-finish oil-based paint, sprays		Wash carefully	Wash carefully

Stenciled fabrics

Different fabrics have different levels of absorbency, may be closely or loosely woven, and have different textures. Absorbency, weave, and texture significantly affect the appearance of the stenciled paint. The examples below show some of these differences. Always test the fabric first to check the effect.

COARSE FABRIC   **CHINTZ**

WHITE CURTAIN FABRIC

CREAM CURTAIN FABRIC

WHITE MUSLIN

CREAM MUSLIN

CALICO

Tiles

Tiles generally are installed in hard-wear areas that need regular cleaning, such as kitchens and bathrooms. These areas also often are steamy. So the paint used for stenciling tiles in kitchens and baths has to be able to withstand these tough conditions. Ceramic paints are the ideal choice. Use cold-cure ceramic paints that dry and become hard at room temperature; other ceramic paints must be fired in a kiln before use. On matte tiles, you also can use oil-based paint, but only if the area receives light use and rarely needs intensive cleaning.

*For safe use of spray adhesive, see page 18.

Painting glazed tiles
TOOLS: Stencil, soft stencil brush
MATERIALS: Spray adhesive,* masking tape, ceramic paints, palette

Painting matte tiles
TOOLS: Stencil, soft stencil brush
MATERIALS: Spray adhesive, masking tape, oil-based stencil crayons, palette

PAINTING GLAZED TILES

1 Clean the tiles if necessary, spray adhesive over the back of the stencil, and position it (see pages 28–29). Add short lengths of masking tape to hold it in place. If the stenciled design covers grouting, apply water-based varnish through the stencil to seal the grout.

2 Using a gentle stippling motion (see Stenciling Techniques, page 31) and a soft stencil brush, apply a small amount of cold-cure ceramic paint. Gradually build up the color in some areas to create shading but do this using the same color of paint; ceramic paint takes too long to dry to add different colors to one area.

3 Be careful when removing the stencil because the paint smudges easily. When the stenciling is complete, let the paints dry and cure completely. This will take about two days.

SOFT BRUSHES
Don't use hard-bristled brushes to apply ceramic paints; they leave brush marks.

PAINTING MATTE TILES

1 Clean the tiles with a detergent solution, then dry well. Spray adhesive over the back of the stencil and position it carefully. Add short lengths of masking tape to hold it in place if necessary (see pages 28–29).

2 Prepare the paint from the stencil crayons (see Steps 1–4 on pages 32–33) and apply it with a gentle stippling motion, building up the color gradually. Add new colors, blending them with the first color to produce a soft, subtle effect.

3 Remove the stencil with care because the paint will still be wet. Don't use the area for at least a day (preferably three to four days), allowing the paint to become completely hard.

Projects

You can stencil many different surfaces and items by adapting the step-by-step techniques already shown in this book. Although you may be tempted to decorate your walls, floors, rugs, blinds, lampshades, fire screen, and all of your glass and ceramic containers to match, be careful not to overdo it.

Start by decorating just a few items, and pick several stencils with the same theme, rather than using the same stencil over and over. Rooms where you relax, such as the living room and bedrooms, can suffer from too much stenciling, but you can afford to experiment more in areas where you stay for shorter periods of time—such as the hall, stairway, landing, and bathroom. Soon you'll develop your own sense of style and repertoire of favorite motifs.

This chapter contains

Room friezes   60
Grouped stencils   62
Blinds and lampshades   64
Rugs and mats   66
Fire screen   68
Containers   70
Cakes   72

Room friezes

In a room where you need a bold image, use a large stencil and repeat it at intervals across the walls. Then combine these shapes with a coordinating pattern that forms a bridge between the large designs to create a spectacular frieze. This is a great way to cheer up a plain bathroom or embellish an otherwise empty staircase.

A large frieze works well below a chair rail, at the top of a wall to visually lower a too-high ceiling, or as a border around a large expanse of wood floor. Always make a sample before you begin working on the actual surface so you can check the position of the design and choose the right colors.

*For safe use of spray adhesive, see page 18.

TOOLS: Large stencil, smaller stencil to join designs, chalk, stencil brushes

MATERIALS: Drop cloths, spray adhesive,* masking tape, water-based stencil paint, palette

1 Take time to work out the area to be stenciled. In a room with floor-standing cabinets and furniture, first plan and mark the position of each large stencil design. The spaces between can be filled in with repeats of the smaller stencil design.

2 Spray adhesive over the back of the main stencil and attach it in the first position. Use a drop cloth to protect the floor below, and lay out all of the paints you'll need.

3 Apply the first color (see pages 30–31) on all areas of the stencil. It's best to use a light color first; it acts as a highlight and forms a good base for the other colors. Here, pale orange paint was used.

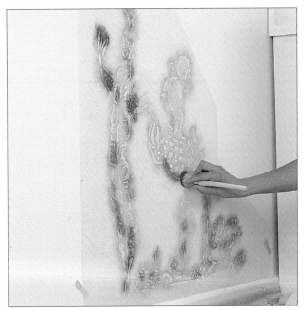

4 Add subsequent deeper colors for contrast and shading. Shade on top of your base color by carefully building up darker layers of color (see Step 4 on page 31).

5 When you've finished, peel the stencil back partially to check your work. Recolor any areas if necessary, then remove the stencil and attach it in the second position to repeat as before.

6 With all the large stencils in place, add the smaller fill-in design. Use the same colors for both stencils. Where only partial sections of the stencil will fit the space, mask over the rest with masking tape.

7 When the stenciling is complete, remove the final stencil. Stand back to check your work, then clean off any paint that may have smudged onto door trim or baseboards.

Grouped stencils

Use a single stencil repeatedly or a group of two or three stencils with the same theme to add even more interest to bare sections of wall. In this pattern, single fish are grouped together to form their own schools.

The best way to make sure you group your stencils correctly and choose the best colors for them is to make a sample. When you're happy with the arrangement and colors, you can start work on the wall confident that your results will be everything you'd hoped they'd be.

*For safe use of spray adhesive, see page 18.

TOOLS: Single stencil or stencils with a theme, stencil brushes, metal rule, stepladder if necessary

MATERIALS: Chalk, spray adhesive,* masking tape, water-based stencil paint, palette

1 Choose areas of blank wall for your design, and mark the position of each stencil in the group. Spray adhesive over the back of the first stencil and attach it in the first position on the wall. Complete this stencil (see pages 30–31).

2 Peel back the stencil and check the colors. Adjust it if necessary. Replace the stencil to repaint the design in the second marked position, then in any other positions until the design is complete.

3 When the group is complete, compare the separate stencils and adjust if necessary.

SOURCES OF INSPIRATION
When stenciling natural objects, use drawings and photographs for inspiration on where and how to shade your designs.

COLOR APPLICATION
Don't be tempted to keep dabbing on paint to a stencil or you could ruin the effect. Peel back the stencil, stand back to check your results, and add more paint only if it's really necessary.

4 These walls were decorated with stencils of the same style and theme to cover the entire area. Plan the main design before you start work. When you've got your plan set out, stand back to check the overall effect and add sections where they'll improve the design. For further inspiration, refer to "Ideas and Choices" (pages 6–13).

Blinds and lampshades

You can stencil purchased fabric items of cotton and polyester if you use water-based stencil paints and if they require only infrequent laundering. Stenciling is a simple way to enhance plain blinds, lampshades, and curtains, including shower curtains. When stenciling over a dark-colored background, brush white stencil paint through the stencil cutouts to block out the background color. Then apply subsequent colors to this base coat.

Roller blind
TOOLS: Stencils, soft stencil brushes

MATERIALS: Drop cloth, spray adhesive, masking tape, water-based stencil paints, palette

Lampshade
TOOLS: Stencils, soft stencil brushes

MATERIALS: Drop cloth, spray adhesive,* masking tape, water-based stencil paints, palette

*For safe use of spray adhesive, see page 18.

ROLLER BLIND

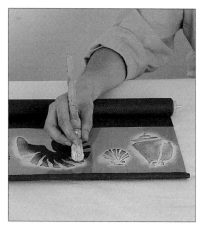

1 Lay the blind over the drop cloth on a table. If necessary, remove the wooden dowel at the blind base and the cord holder. Spray the back of the stencil with adhesive; position and smooth it.

2 If the fabric color is dark, first apply white stencil paint to the complete stencil design, using a swirling motion (see Stenciling Techniques, page 31).

3 After you've done this, peel back part of the stencil to check that all areas have been painted. When you're satisfied, let this first coat of paint dry for a few minutes.

4 Paint the design. When the stencil is removed, the colors applied over the white background will show up better—even ones similar to the color of the blind.

5 When the paint is completely dry, replace the dowel and cord holder, and hang the blind.

LAMPSHADE

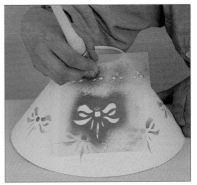

1 Spray the back of the stencil with adhesive and smooth it onto the shade. Use strips of masking tape to hold each corner of the stencil in place. Stand back and check that the stencil is correctly positioned.

2 With the soft brush and paint, apply the first color using swirling strokes. Use the brush almost dry, and build up coats as highlights using the stippling method (see Stenciling Techniques, page 31).

3 When you've finished the first design and the paint is dry, position the second stencil and apply the paint for it in the same way.

4 This simple stencil design turns a plain lamp and shade into a colorful accessory that you can decorate to coordinate or contrast with other furnishings in the room.

SHADY PRACTICE
If you incorrectly plan where to place the design on the shade so the shapes aren't evenly spaced, adapt your original design idea by adding extra elements from the stencils to fill in and hide the mistake.

Rugs and mats

Natural-fiber rugs and mats make good candidates for stenciling. Here, spray paint is best because it sinks into the fibers and won't loosen them—something that's difficult to accomplish with a brush.

*For safe use of spray adhesive and aerosol spray paints, see pages 18 and 21.

Cotton rug
TOOLS: Stencils

MATERIALS: Spray adhesive,* masking tape, lining paper or newspaper, aerosol spray paints,* drop cloth

Mat
TOOLS: Stencils

MATERIALS: Spray adhesive,* masking tape, lining paper or newspaper, aerosol spray paints,* drop cloth, clear varnish

COTTON RUG

1 Using a clean brush and dustpan, brush the rug to make sure it's free of loose fibers. Then vacuum up any small stray fibers. Lay the rug flat over the drop cloth to protect the floor surface underneath it.

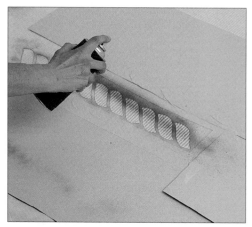

2 Plan the design and position the first stencil. Mask out the rest of the rug with lining paper taped to the stencil with masking tape (to avoid overspray). Apply the first color (see Step 1 on page 34).

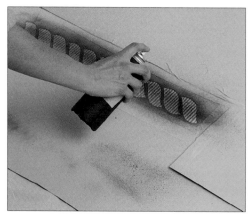

3 Spray on your second color as a highlight, building up the color gradually (see steps 2–3 on page 34). If the color becomes too strong, apply a lighter shade of the same color to soften it. Move the stencil, and mask it in the second position for painting.

4 When the border is finished and dry, apply the central motifs. The colors will fade in time, but even this has its own charm. See the Brighten Up box, below.

COLOR TEST
Test how colors react with the material by trying them out on the back of the rug. Don't use this test on an open-weave rug, however; color may bleed through the surface and show up on the exposed side.

MAT

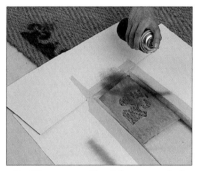

1 Make sure the mat is clean and free of loose fibers. Lay the mat on a drop cloth on the floor or a table. Plan the design, deciding how close to the edges the border should go. An ideal distance for a 2×3-foot mat is about 2 inches.

2 Spray the back of the stencil with adhesive and smooth it in the first position. Mask an area around the stencil at least 12 inches on each side. Use masking tape to attach it to the stencil. Apply the first color (see Step 1 on page 34), then the second.

3 Use a stencil with an angled design for neat corners, or miter the design (see page 43). Use light pressure on the nozzle and keep the can moving. For continuity, keep your color depth the same in each area.

4 When you've finished the border, stand back and check your work. If you need to make adjustments, follow the steps on pages 36–37, as appropriate. The mat is now ready to use and enjoy.

BRIGHTEN UP
To set the design and maintain its color intensity, apply spray varnish over the surface when the design is complete. Oil-based varnish may look better on yellow or brown mats.

Fire screen

Medium-density fiberboard (MDF) is an ideal material for a fire screen because it's so easy to shape. Draw a template on paper for the main screen and a separate one for the feet, then ask your lumberyard to cut out the shapes for you. The main screen is glued into the slots in the feet. Choose a design to complement the screen shape and the style of your room. This screen was first painted with water-based paint, and then a coat of color wash was added. Use a pale color for the base coat and a stronger color for the wash so it will show against the pale background.

*For safe use of spray adhesive, see page 18.

TOOLS: Stencil, stencil brushes, synthetic sponge, household paintbrushes

MATERIALS: Vinyl matte emulsion, fine-grit sandpaper, water-based paint for color washing, spray adhesive,* masking tape, water-based stencil paint, palette, water-based clear varnish

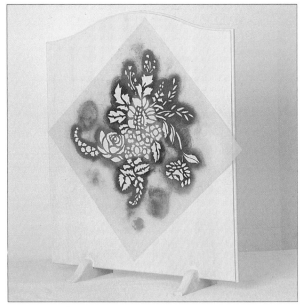

1 Paint the screen with three coats of paint. Allow it to dry, and sand lightly between coats. Mix the paint for the color washing. Dilute 1 part paint to 10–15 parts water. Check the color on paper and add more water if necessary. Sponge on the color wash.

2 When the color wash is dry, apply spray adhesive to the stencil and center it on the screen. Apply the first color (see pages 30–31). You may find it easier to lay the screen flat as in Step 4, opposite. Work quickly but carefully.

3 Add highlights and shadows (see Step 4 on page 31). Partially remove the stencil to check the results. If any alterations are needed, carefully reposition the stencil and make them (see pages 36–37). Remove the stencil.

4 If the design needs filling in, reposition the stencil to add extra flowers, leaves, or any other design element. Mask out the surrounding areas that you don't want to include before you add paint to the newly positioned shapes.

5 When you're done, varnish the screen to protect it. Use two or three coats of water-based varnish, applied with a household paintbrush according to the manufacturer's instructions.

GUARANTEE THE RIGHT RESULTS
To make sure you'll be delighted with your results, check your design first. Using a sheet of paper, draw around the outline of the screen and cut out the shape. Stencil the complete color design on the paper, then cut it out and stick it to the front of the fire screen. Live with it for a few days and adjust it if necessary.

Containers

Although you can stencil glass or ceramic containers with almost any paint, the surface soon will wear off if you used anything but cold-cure ceramic paints. They not only work well on bottles and pots, but they also can be used to decorate windows, mirrors, and tiles.

Glass jar
TOOLS: Stencils, soft stencil brush

MATERIALS: Container, spray adhesive, masking tape, cardboard, cold-cure ceramic paints, drop cloth, solvent

Terra-cotta pots
TOOLS: Household paintbrush, stencils, soft stencil brushes

MATERIALS: Pots, pale household water-based paint, spray adhesive,* masking tape, water-based stencil paints, palette

*For safe use of spray adhesive, see page 18.

GLASS JAR

1 Thoroughly wash and dry the surface to be stenciled to remove all grease and dust. Spray the back of the stencil with adhesive and position it as required. Use masking-tape strips at the corners of the stencil to make sure it doesn't slip.

2 Apply the first color in ceramic paint, using the brush in a stippling motion (see Stenciling Techniques, page 31) to achieve soft, even results. Add the second color almost immediately but be careful not to smudge the paint. It's not practical to wait for the first coat to dry since ceramic paints take 6 hours to dry to the touch and days to get completely hard.

3 Carefully remove the stencil to avoid smudging the paint edges. If you're not happy with your results, remove the paint with solvent, dry the surface well, and repeat the stenciling. If your mistake is an easy one to fix, let the paint dry and then make any corrections. (See the chart on pages 36–37.)

4 Use stencils of a similar theme to coordinate a variety of different-shaped bottles and jars. Wrap a stencil around a curved jar and attach it with masking tape. Stencil each surface individually on containers with flat surfaces, and remember to remove the masking tape as soon as your stenciling is complete. It can be difficult to remove if you let paint dry on it (see Step 5 on page 29).

TERRA-COTTA POTS AND SAUCERS

Cover a terra-cotta pot and its saucer with a coat of pale water-based paint. Then color-wash over this with a contrasting color as you did for the fire screen (see Step 1 on page 68). When it's dry, decorate it with a stenciled design using the same technique as for the glass jar. Set the paint by brushing all surfaces with water-based varnish.

WALL CUPBOARD

On a glass-front cupboard or door, you can create the look of etched glass. Attach a reverse-cutout shape (the area in a stencil that's normally removed) on the inside of the glass, adhering it with spray adhesive. Then, using white oil-based primer, stipple the glass on the inside (see Stenciling Techniques, page 31). When the reverse-cutout shape is removed, this area will appear as a transparent window.

Cakes

Now here's a stencil design that takes the cake—or should we say *makes* the cake. Just use edible food coloring, available in liquid and other forms. We mixed a powdered form with water to make a thick liquid we applied over the cake icing. If you use liquid food coloring, be careful not to overload the brush; wipe it on a paper towel until it's nearly dry before you start to apply the stencil design.

TOOLS: Stencils and small, soft stencil brush

MATERIALS: Sugar-and-water syrup solution (optional, since it can tint the icing), palette, liquid food coloring, waxed paper

1 Place the cake to be decorated on waxed paper on a flat surface. Because you can't use spray adhesive to hold the stencil in place, use a thin coat of syrup solution instead, or simply hold down the stencil with your hand.

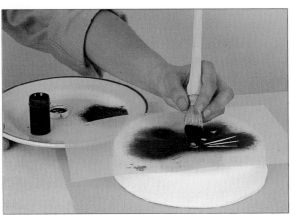

2 Apply the food coloring with a soft, almost-dry brush, and paint them on using a swirling motion (see Stenciling Techniques, page 31).

3 When the design on the cake top is complete, carefully remove the stencil. Let the coloring dry before going on to the next stage.

4 For the sides, plan the spacing you need between each stencil. Keep the cake at a slight angle while you apply the design. Hold the stencil and cake in one hand, and apply the coloring with a brush in the other hand. Move stencil and cake around as you work, then let the side motifs dry.

5 Decorate the cake with bows, balls, and ribbons, or simply leave it stenciled. Even though it probably looks too good to eat, go on and dig in.

STILL MORE CAKE DESIGNS

Naturally attractive
For a nature enthusiast, use stenciled butterflies, flowers, leaf patterns, or other motifs from nature around a central sprig.

Dog-day decor
Make a cake for pet lovers using a stencil design, complete with bows, of their favorite breed of dog, cat, or other animal.

DECORATING IDEAS
There are so many different ways you can decorate a cake with stencils. Build up a three-dimensional design by stenciling icing that's been rolled flat. Just cut out the shapes and use syrup solution to stick them onto a cake with plain icing. Or, use a sprayer (see page 23) and food-coloring markers to come up with an intricate, one-of-a-kind design.

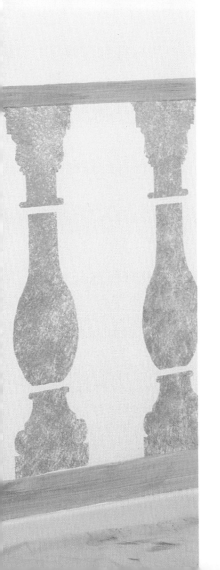

Creating Illusions

Besides using stencils to create borders, friezes, and grouped motifs, you can design complete wall treatments and create illusions. Stencils are wonderful for letting you furnish your rooms in ways you really don't have the space or the money for.

Trompe l'oeil designs are used to deliberately fool the eye with realistic images. They let you enjoy dream views of vast palatial gardens, antique furniture, wildlife, pets, or anything else that appeals to you and your sense of humor.

This chapter contains

Plate shelf	76
Hanging basket	78
Garden balustrade	80

Plate shelf

In a confined space, such as a small entry, kitchen, or landing, there's little room for furniture or wall-hung displays. But there's lots of room for a trompe l'oeil effect.

Stencil a shelf holding a decorative collection of glass or ceramics on the wall, create a group of wall-hung plates, or add a painted dresser complete with a set of matching china. These and many other effects are easy with stencils.

TOOLS: Steel rule, level, chalk, stencils, stencil brushes, stepladder

MATERIALS: Drop cloths, spray adhesive,* masking tape, water-based stencil paint, palette

*For safe use of spray adhesive, see page 18.

1 Use the rule, level, and chalk to mark the position for the shelf. Cut a simple shelf-shaped stencil, making the shelf about 2 inches deep, then add short brackets about 4 inches in from each end for a shelf like the one shown here (see "Designing and Cutting Stencils," pages 82–91). The shelf on this wall is about 3 feet long; for a longer shelf, add a center bracket.

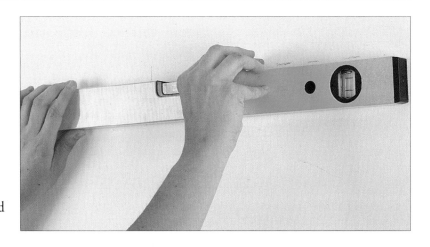

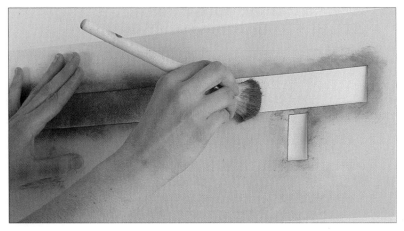

2 Here, the shelf is stenciled in brown, using a sweeping motion that imitates wood grain. You also could color the shelf to match other items in the room, or stencil shelves all around the room. For a shorter shelf, simply decrease the width of the shelf and the length of the brackets. Look at real shelves and brackets to determine lengths and widths.

3 When you've finished the shelf and brackets, attach the stencils for the plates, bowls, and glasses you'd like to "display" on the shelf. Group them close together or space them out along the entire shelf.

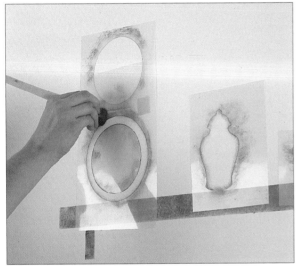

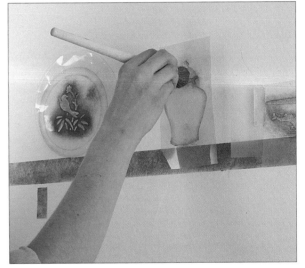

4 The outer edge of a plate is stenciled as a faint shadow of blue, applied with an almost-dry brush. Brush in a circle on the stencil, allowing only part of the brush to touch the wall to give the effect of a plate rim as shown in Step 5.

5 Add a center plate design of your choice as a second stencil, applying it with a brush (see page 31). Complete the crockery set, adding shading at edges as shown in Step 4. Match the designs to create a set or mix them for variety.

6 The final stenciled design looks just like a collection of ceramics sitting on a shelf. For an even more realistic look, spend time creating the effect of light and shadow falling on the shelf and its contents (see Step 4 on page 31).

Hanging basket

The main disadvantage of a real hanging basket is that it requires watering and seasonal replanting. And if you don't care for it, you could end up with pests and dead plants. Stencil your containers instead, indoors or out, and fill them with whatever plants you'd like to flower forever without further attention.

*For safe use of spray adhesive, see page 18.

TOOLS: Steel rule, level, chalk, stencils, natural sea sponge, stencil brushes, stepladder

MATERIALS: Drop cloths, spray adhesive,* masking tape, water-based stencil paints, palette, plate

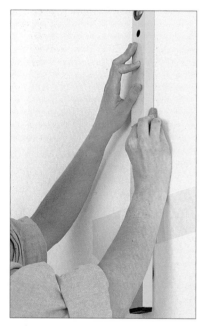

1 Mark a horizontal chalk line for the position of the top of the basket liner. Check your accuracy with the level, then spray the back of the liner stencil and press it to the wall. From the center of the liner top, mark a vertical line to the point where the hanging wires will meet.

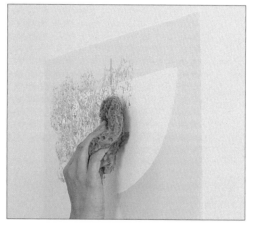

2 Stencil the shape of the basket liner using a natural sea sponge and a gentle dabbing motion; apply greens, browns, and a little pale orange to imitate moss (see Steps 1–3 on page 35).

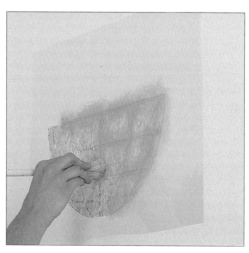

3 Use a second stencil positioned over the first for the wires of the basket. To make the wires show up clearly, use a contrasting shade or a totally different color. Green was used here but black would be just as good.

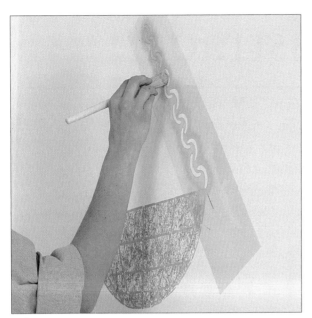

4 The hanging wires run from the top of the central vertical line to join the basket at each side. Apply paint with the stencil brush, using the same color as for the wire basket.

5 Attach the plant stencil and use white paint to cover areas where the leaves will spill over the basket (see Steps 2–3 on page 64). Let the white paint dry.

6 Apply the true colors for the leaves. Build up the colors to simulate real leaves. Add more leaves as needed, using sections of the existing stencil and masking out areas that you don't want to include. Let the paint dry.

IVY LEAGUE

Later, you may want to add more climbing and trailing ivy or even entire extra plants— whatever embellishments work best with your original design. Let additional ivy strands wind up the hanging wires and trail farther down the basket sides.

Garden balustrade

If one of your rooms lacks an interesting view, why not use stencils to transform a plain wall into the view of your dreams? Here, an ornate stone balustrade was topped with ivy-filled decorative urns. To add interest, use stencils to create the garden you've always wanted, whether it's a formal rose or herb garden, hedges decorated like a topiary, or even a lake or river abundant with birds and leaping fish. The simple design shown here works well in a hallway or on any other large expanse of wall.

*For safe use of spray adhesive, see page 18.

TOOLS: Steel rule, level, chalk, stencil, natural sea sponge, stencil brushes

MATERIALS: Drop cloths, spray adhesive,* masking tape, water-based stencil paints, palette, plate

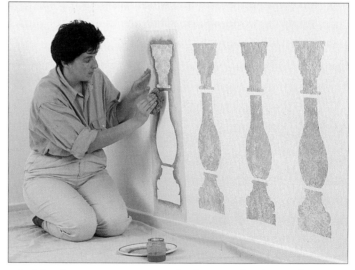

1 Work out the spacing for the balustrade uprights and the urns on the top rail so they'll fit the wall space you have available. Mark their positions with chalk. Allow room for a balustrade base directly above the baseboard. Apply spray adhesive to the stencil, and position the first upright, using a level to ensure it's perfectly vertical.

2 Use the sea sponge to apply the stencil paint with a gentle dabbing motion (see Steps 1–3 on page 35). This technique will simulate the texture of stone when seen from a distance. Sponge brown paint over yellow to imitate sandstone, or brown paint over gray for fieldstone. You can add green in some areas for moss. For an added touch, work out the angle of an imaginary sun, including the light and shadows it would throw on the scene.

3 When all uprights are complete, add the top and bottom rails. Lightly chalk in two parallel lines the width of each rail, and apply detacked masking tape (see Step 5 on page 29) along the outside of each line. Sponge the rails as you did the uprights. Remove the tape as soon as possible.

4 When the paint on the top rail is dry, position the first urn and sponge it to match the balustrade. Add light and shadows (see Step 4 on page 31) as you did for the uprights. Repeat for all urns.

5 Add ivy or the flowers of your choice to match your room scheme. Where greenery or flowers trail over the container, stencil in white first to mask the urn color, then stencil the final colors.

6 The finished balustrade and urns added just the right touch to this room. Just for fun, consider adding birds, butterflies, ladybugs, bees, and even caterpillars. Later you could include a distant view, stenciled in pale receding colors to suggest its perspective.

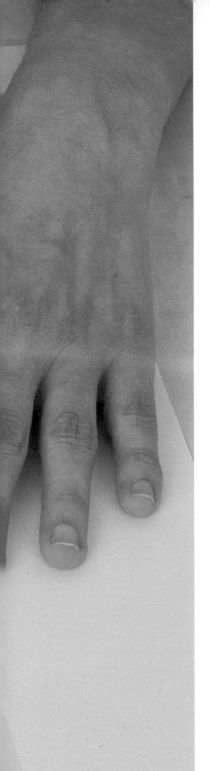

Designing and Cutting Stencils

You may find that commercial stencil designs eventually limit your creativity. Once you've perfected your stenciling skills, you'll almost certainly want to broaden your repertoire. And you can broaden it to your heart's content by designing and cutting your own stencils, which will be inexpensive as well as unique.

You don't have to be an artist to design your own stencils; you can duplicate designs found on fabric in the room, use photographs and illustrations as sources, or copy images from nature.

Stencils are designed in three ways: Single-layer stencils have all colors and shapes on one stencil, outlined and divided by narrow bridges of stencil material; multiple-layer stencils use a separate sheet for each color; and detailing stencils are used to add intricate detail to a previously stenciled design.

This chapter contains

Single-layer stencils	84
Multiple-layer stencils	86
Using a crafts knife	88
Using a hot-knife cutter	90

Single-layer stencils

On single-layer stencils, the complete design, including any details, is all on one sheet. Because you need divisions between colors and shapes—if you cut all the way around an object, the middle will drop out—single-layer stencils have thin connecting strips of stencil material called bridges. These bridges give the finished design a distinctive stenciled appearance and also help keep the stencil from becoming distorted during use. The hardest part of creating a single-layer stencil is deciding where to put these bridges. Look carefully at commercial stencils before deciding where your bridges should go.

If you're creating an original design, plan it carefully on a piece of paper. You may find it also helps to color in your design. An outline of any one shape or color usually is defined by a bridge. But you also can use bridges to add various kinds of details, such as the veins on a leaf.

TOOLS: Fabric piece, solvent-based waterproof pen, stencil brush

MATERIALS: Tracing paper, stencil material, water-based stencil paint

1 Enlarge or reduce your original design on a photocopier until it's the correct size. Photocopying also helps to highlight the shadows, which is where bridges should go.

2 Position a sheet of tracing paper over the design and trace the design onto it. Use the divisions between colors to form bridges. Bridges should be no narrower than ¹⁄₁₆ inch when used to divide intricate designs and wider on bolder shapes.

3 Next look at areas within colors where shadows fall, and use them for more bridges as necessary. Shade the areas to be cut out to make sure that one area doesn't bleed into another and that the stencil won't fall apart.

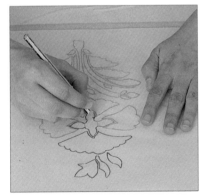

4 Trace the design onto the stencil material to be used, and cut out the stencil. (See pages 88–91 for instructions on cutting out the different types of stencil material.) If you happen to make a mistake at this point by leaving out an important part of the stencil, add it as a detailing stencil (see page 87).

5 Test the finished effect by making a sample on paper. Compare the finished stencil with the fabric pattern and make any adjustments that are necessary. The stencil is now ready to use.

BUILDING BRIDGES

Bridges should appear at regular intervals to keep your design intact.

To practice locating bridges, draw and cut a simple design in different ways to see what positions work best. It's worth taking the time to get the design right at this stage.

Bold designs need fewer but wider bridges than intricate shapes. Use the contours of a design as bridges to highlight the shape, such as the veins of a leaf or the divisions between the petals of a flower.

Multiple-layer stencils

Multiple-layer stencils usually consist of a separate layer for each color that's used in the stencil. This type of stencil doesn't need bridges to divide areas, but it's still important to be able to line up each stencil accurately so the various colors and shapes on each sheet appear in their corresponding positions.

To do this, use dotted lines to outline all shapes on the other stencils, together with the cutout shapes on the stencil you're using. Then, when you position the stencil, match up the dotted outlines to the sections of the design you've already stenciled, and add the new color through the cutouts. A detailing stencil is placed over an area you've already stenciled to add intricate shapes to the design.

TOOLS: Fabric piece, solvent-based waterproof pen, stencil brush

MATERIALS: Stencil material, tracing paper, water-based stencil paint

1 When using a design copied from a piece of fabric, enlarge or reduce the pattern area on a photocopier until it's the correct size. Color in the design, using a separate stencil sheet for each color. With very complicated designs, this can mean using up to ten different stencils.

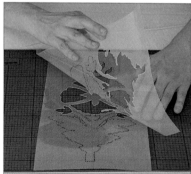

2 On each sheet of stencil material, trace the complete design. Use a dotted line for all the shapes you won't cut out, and a solid line for shapes you will cut out. The continuous lines will appear in different places on each stencil sheet. Cut along the solid lines (see pages 88–91).

3 Position and apply paint through the cutouts on one stencil (see pages 30–35), using the first color.

4 Apply the second color through the cutout shapes in the second stencil in the same way, making sure you line up the dotted lines with the first color outlines. Repeat for all other colors.

DETAILING STENCILS

1 To add delicate details, use a separate stencil. Again, mark the main outline with a dotted line, and the detail shapes with a solid line. Then cut along the solid lines.

2 Carefully line up the detail stencil over the main stencil where the colors already have been applied.

3 Add details using a darker or lighter shade of the original color so they're clear, or choose different colors for a complete and total contrast.

4 You can produce some sophisticated and intricate effects using a number of overlays and one or more separate-color detailing stencils.

5 This design shows the levels of intricacy you can achieve with a detailing stencil.

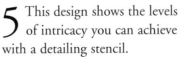

Using a crafts knife

When using a crafts knife to cut polyester or oiled stencil card, apply pressure on the knife evenly to control it; it can slip easily. Use the knife in one long, continuous movement, and move the stencil as you follow the shape you're cutting.

Although you can substitute a vinyl tile or even a magazine, a special cutting mat makes the job much easier and helps you control the knife.

TOOLS: Crafts knife, resealable cutting mat, solvent-based waterproof pen

MATERIALS: Stencil design, stencil material

CUTTING STENCIL CARD

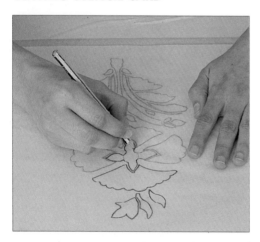

1 Transfer the design onto the stencil material using a reverse tracing technique. First trace the design onto tracing paper. Then place the drawn side down on top of the card stock and use a pencil to retrace the design.

2 Use the pen to go over the light outline you made so the design is clearer. Compare it with the design on the fabric.

3 Place the stencil on top of the cutting mat. Holding the knife in one hand as you would a pencil, use the other hand to control the stencil. Pierce the stencil material and move the stencil so you're cutting in long, smooth, continuous sweeps, always working toward yourself.

4 Remove each cutout shape as you finish working on it. If you accidentally cut through a bridge, mend the stencil (see page 25).

CUTTING SURFACES

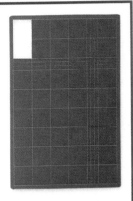

As a cutting surface, a resealable cutting mat is expensive but invaluable if you plan to make a lot of stencils.

You can substitute a thick magazine or a vinyl tile, but each of these surfaces should be used only once.

CUTTING TRANSPARENT POLYESTER

1 In this case, trace the design directly onto the transparent polyester. Place the stencil sheet over the design and draw in the lines with the solvent-based marking pen.

2 Use a hot-knife cutter if you have one or a crafts knife in the same way you'd use it to cut card stock (see Step 3, page 88). Once more, a cutting mat offers much better control and reduces the possibility of mistakes.

HOT-KNIFE CUTTERS

By far the easiest way to cut transparent polyester is to use a hot-knife stencil cutter (see pages 90–91). It melts the material and is similar to using a pen, although slower. It requires little pressure, and the tip isn't difficult to control, making it a practically foolproof tool for cutting stencils.

Using a hot-knife cutter

The hot-knife stencil cutter has revolutionized cutting polyester and acetate stencils. The cutter has a hot tip that melts the material as it glides over it and requires little effort to control. A crafts knife, on the other hand, requires a certain amount of pressure and precise control. To protect the surface underneath the stencil when using a hot-knife cutter, always place a sheet of glass under the stencil.

TOOLS: Polyester or acetate stencil material, hot-knife stencil cutter

MATERIALS: Sheet of polished-edge plate glass larger than the stencil

1 Using a solvent-based permanent marking pen, copy the design onto the polyester or acetate. Place the stencil sheet over the glass. You may find it helpful to put the original under the glass, using it as a reference.

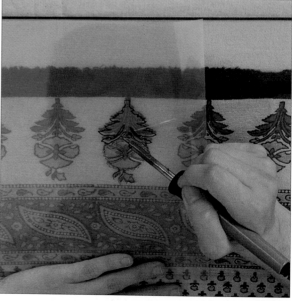

2 Practice on a spare piece of stencil material first, then cut the stencil. Hold the hot-knife stencil cutter upright by the handle, with the side of your hand resting on the cutting surface. This helps keep your hand steady. Gently and slowly, cut through the stencil material in clean sweeps. If the knife skids, you're going over the surface too fast. A skid won't damage the stencil, however.

3 After peeling back the transparent polyester, the cutout pieces will remain stuck to the glass, leaving a cleanly cut stencil that's ready to use.

4 When you use this cutter, the cutout shapes appear similar to those cut with a crafts knife, but there's a fine ridge around the cut edges where the transparent polyester has melted. Excessive buildup of this ridge is caused by holding the cutter at too much of an angel. This buildup won't. interfere with using the stencil, though; in fact, in some cases it actually strengthens the stencil design.

CUTTING STENCILS FROM ORIGINALS

When you become adept at using a hot-knife cutter, you can cut a design directly from an original by placing the original below the sheet of plate glass.

Make sure you work directly above the design or you may get some distortion through the thickness of the glass. Be especially careful to include bridges in single-layer stencils. If you need to alter the design to include them, it's better to trace it and then adjust your tracing as necessary. Ink in the final design using a solvent-based marking pen, and continue as shown.

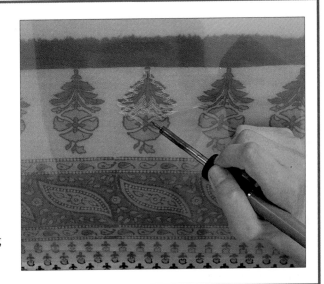

Glossary

Aerosol
A canister holding vapor as liquid under pressure; some paints and repositioning adhesives come in aerosol form.

Air Marker
A hand-held tool that, when pressed, emits paint blown from the end of a felt tip.

Bleeding
Paint that seeps under the edge of a stencil.

Border
A repeating band of stencils that can be positioned at any height and on almost any surface.

Bridges
Narrow strips between open areas of a stencil that hold it together.

Buildup
Paint that sometimes accumulates at the edges of stencils.

Chalk line
A line drawn onto a surface to help position the stencil accurately.

Color wash
A thin coat of paint and water applied to create a subtle surface texture and color.

Cure
The period of chemical change when paint hardens to provide a tough, waterproof surface.

Cutouts
Areas removed for application of paint when a stencil is cut.

Detack
To remove some stickiness from a surface. Masking tape should be applied to a clean fabric a number of times before it's applied to a wall so it doesn't damage the wall surface when it's removed.

Dilute
To thin paint with a suitable solvent to make it less concentrated.

Domed-end brush
A stencil brush with bristles that are rounded at the working end.

Frieze
Similar to a border, a decorative band usually applied horizontally to a wall.

Guide marks
Chalk or pencil marks that help you position a stencil correctly.

Highlight

Additional light or dark colors added to a stencil to create the effect of natural lighting.

Horizontal parallel

A line level with the ground.

Line up

To make one stencil match the position of another.

Mask

To apply protection around a stencil to prevent overspray.

Miter

A diagonal joint across the corner where two border pieces meet at a right angle.

Multiple-layer stencil

A stenciled design that uses more than one stencil.

Parallel

Two lines that always remain the same distance apart.

Polyester

A strong, transparent stencil material.

Repositioning spray adhesive

A low-tack spray glue that allows for stencil repositioning.

Seepage

Paint that leaks under a stencil.

Single-layer stencil

A stencil design that uses only one stencil.

Stippling

A stenciling method in which paint is applied in an up-and-down pouncing motion to produce textured results.

Swirling

A stenciling method in which paint is applied in a circular motion to produce smooth, soft results.

Template

A pattern used as a guide when cutting.

Trompe l'oeil

Literally, something that fools the eye. A painted scene or effect that simulates real life.

Index

acetate 17, 90

acrylic plastic 40, 41

adhesive 18, 29, 93

aerosols 21, 23, 34, 45, 92

air marker 23, 92

applications *see* projects;
    surfaces

applicators 22-3

base surfaces 40-1

bathroom 11

bedroom 8-9

bleeding 30, 34, 53, 92

blinds 54, 64-5

borders 29, 92
    floors 48-9
    rugs 66-7
    walls 8-9, 42-3

brass 17

brick 40, 41, 44

bridges 24, 84, 85, 91, 92

brushes 22, 24, 30, 57

buildup 92

cakes 40, 72-3

ceramic containers 70

ceramic paints 39, 40, 56, 70

chalk line 19, 28, 92

cleaning
    stencils 24, 25
    tools 15, 20, 24

color fading 33

color wash 50, 68, 71, 92

containers 70-1

copying designs 84, 86, 91

corners, mitered 43

correction tape 19, 25

crafts knife 18, 88-9

crayons 21, 32-3, 57

curing 21, 41, 70, 92

curtains 11, 54

cutouts 92

cutting mats 18, 19, 89

cutting stencils 88-91

designing stencils 82-7, 91

detacking 29, 92

detailing stencils 16, 87

diluting 92

domed-end brush 22, 92

doors 13, 45-7

drafting film 17

equipment 18-19

fabrics 11, 41, 52-5
    blinds 64-5
    lampshades 65
    paints 20, 39, 40, 54
    rugs and mats 66-7

finishes 23

fire screen 68-9

floors 48-9
    rugs and mats 9, 66-7

friezes 10, 60-1, 92

furniture 13, 50-1
    bedroom 8
    kitchen 10, 71

garden balustrade 80-1

glass
    cutting mat 18, 90-1
    designs on 40, 70-1

grouped stencils 52-3

guide marks 19, 92

hanging basket 78-9

highlights 31, 46, 93

horizontal parallel 93

hot-knife stencil cutter 18, 89, 90-1

ideas and choices 6-13

illusions 74-81
    garden balustrade 80-1
    hanging basket 78-9
    plate shelf 76-7

kitchen 10-11

lampshades 54, 65

large areas 34-5

lining up stencils 93

mask 29, 93

masking tape 18
    detacking 29, 92

materials 14-23

mats 9, 66-7

melamine surfaces 40, 51

mistakes 27, 36-7

miters 43, 93

multiple-layer stencils 16, 86-7, 93

oil-based paint 21, 32-3, 45, 56

oiled stencil card 17, 88

outdoor uses 12

paint

    applications 40

    fabric 20, 39, 40, 54

    method 41

    oil-based 21, 32-3, 45, 56

    problems 36

    using 30-1

    water-based 20

paneling 8, 46-7

parallel 93

pen 18, 90

plate shelf 76-7

polyester 17, 52, 64, 89, 90, 93

positioning stencils 28-9, 52-3

problems 36

projects 58-73

    blinds 64-5

    cakes 72-3

    containers 70-1

    fire screen 68-9

    friezes 60-1

    grouped stencils 52-3

projects *(continued)*

    lampshades 65

    rugs and mats 66-7

protecting designs 10, 21, 33, 67, 69

repairing stencils 25

repositioning spray adhesive 18, 29, 93

rugs 66-7

safety 18, 21

samples 27, 31, 69

securing stencils 35

seepage 36, 37, 93

sheds 12

single-layer stencils 16, 84-5, 93

sponges 23, 34, 35, 78, 80

spray adhesive 18, 29, 93

sprayers 23, 29

spray paint 21, 23, 34, 45, 92

stencils

    cleaning 24, 25

    cutting 88-91

    designing 82-7

    materials 17

    positioning 28-9, 52-3

    repairing 25

    securing 35

    types 16, 84-7

stippling 31, 39, 44, 93

surfaces 28, 38-57

    methods to use 41

    paints 40

    suggestions 12-13

    textured 39, 40, 41, 44

swirling 31, 33, 44, 93

techniques 26-37, 41

template 93

terra-cotta 12, 39, 40, 71

textured surfaces 39, 40, 41, 44

tiles 32, 40, 41, 56-7

tone 31, 46

tools 15, 18-19, 88-91

    cleaning 15, 20, 24

toy box 50-1

tracing paper 19, 85

trompe-l'oeil 75, 76-7, 93

varnish 10, 21, 33, 49, 67, 69

walls 42-4

    bathroom 11

    bedroom 8-9

    borders 42-3

    friezes 10, 60-1, 92

    grouped stencils 62-3

    illusions 74-81

    kitchen 10-11

    textured 44

water-based paints 20

windows 10

wooden surfaces 40, 41, 48-51

Meredith® Press
An imprint of Meredith® Books

Do-It-Yourself Decorating
Step-by-Step Stenciling
Editor, Shelter Books: Denise L. Caringer
Contributing Editor: David A. Kirchner
Contributing Designer: Jeff Harrison
Copy Chief: Angela K. Renkoski

Meredith® Books
Editor in Chief: James D. Blume
Managing Editor: Christopher Cavanaugh
Director, New Product Development: Ray Wolf
Vice President, Retail Sales: Jamie L. Martin

Meredith Publishing Group
President, Publishing Group: Christopher M. Little
Vice President and Publishing Director: John P. Loughlin

Meredith Corporation
Chairman of the Board and Chief Executive Officer: Jack D. Rehm
President and Chief Operating Officer: William T. Kerr
Chairman of the Executive Committee: E. T. Meredith III

First published 1996 by Haynes Publishing

All of us at Meredith® Books are dedicated to providing you with information and ideas you need to enhance your home. We welcome your comments and suggestions about this book on stenciling. Write to us at: Meredith® Books, Do-It-Yourself Editorial Department, RW-206, 1716 Locust St., Des Moines, IA 50309-3023.

This edition published by Meredith Corporation, Des Moines Iowa, 1997
Printed in France
Printing Number and Year: 5 4 3 2 1 00 99 98 97 96
Library of Congress Catalog Card Number: 96-78043
ISBN: 0-696-20679-X